The Romance of Manitoba Settlements

Colin A. Thomson

Calgary, Alberta, Canada

The Romance of Manitoba Settlements
© 2008 Colin Thomson

Library And Archives Canada Cataloging in Publication

Thomson, Colin A., 1938-
The Romance of Manitoba settlements / Colin A. Thomson.

Includes bibliographical references.
ISBN 978-1-55059-350-1

1. Names, Geographical--Manitoba--History. 2. Manitoba -- Biography. I. Title.

FC3356.T46 2008   971.27'0099   C2008-901508-8

210 1220 Kensington Rd NW
Calgary, Ab. T2N 3P5
www.temerondetselig.com

DETSELIG
ENTERPRISES LTD
p. 403-283-0900
f. 403-283-6945
e. temeron@telusplanet.net

All rights reserved. No part of this book can be reproduced in any form or by any means without written permission from the publisher.

We recognize the support of the Government of Canada through the Book Publishing Industry Development Program (BPIDP) for our publishing program.
We also acknowledge the support of the Alberta Foundation for the Arts for our publishing program.

SAN 113-0234
ISBN 978-155059-350-1
Printed in Canada

COMMITTED TO THE DEVELOPMENT OF CULTURE AND THE ARTS

Cover Design by James Dangerous

For **E. M. T.**

Note to the Reader

This book honors certain women and men of the pen (quill) and brush who have had Manitoba settlements named in their honor (although some of those settlements and railway points no longer exist). Call them Manitopens!

They include writers, poets, engineers, historians, surveyors, artists, philosophers, administrators, composers, missionaries, cartographers, geologists, academics, and journalists, among others. As one would expect, some of these individuals demanded more discussion than others.

Other settlements and place names are also noted. Such names remind us of the courage, sacrifice, accomplishments, failures, happiness, sorrow, and atrocities experienced or witnessed by earlier citizens of Manitoba.

Think of such people as Mrs. Julienne Cantin, after whom Cantin Lake was named. All her ten children served in the Canadian armed forces during World War II. This modest endeavor is dedicated to her name, and to so many other people who have made today's Manitoba strong and vibrant.

Acknowledgements

I am grateful to Eleanor Hawthorne, whose technical assistance was cheerfully offered. Efficiently and effectively, James Dangerous added the finishing touches to this endeavor.

Table of Contents

Agassiz *Louis Agassiz*	9
Allegra, Ponemah, and Nokomis Lake *Henry Wadsworth Longfellow*	13
Ami Island *Henri-Marc Ami*	16
Back *George Back*	17
Baden, Powell and Mafeking *Lord Baden-Powell*	18
Begg Lake *Alexander Begg*	19
Belcher *Edward Belcher*	20
Benito *Herman Melville*	22
Beulah *Augusta Jane Evans Wilson*	24
Bonnie Doon *Robert Burns*	25
Bradwardine *Walter Scott*	30
Button *Thomas Button*	33
Bylot *Robert Bylot*	36
Cabot *John Cabot*	38
Carman *Albert Carman*	41
Cauchon Lake *Joseph Édouard Cauchon*	43
Coldwell Lake *William Coldwell*	44
Coleman Island *Arthur P. Coleman*	46
Dafoe Lake *John Wesley Dafoe*	48
Dand *Archibald Lampman*	51
Dennis Lake *John Stoughton Dennis*	55
Dugas *Abbé Georges Dugas*	57
Emerson *Ralph Waldo Emerson*	60

Evans Point	*James Evans*	64
Falcon Lake	*Pierre Falcon*	66
Flin Flon	*Flinty*	68
Fort Garry	*Nicholas Garry*	69
Franklin	*Sir John Franklin*	72
Gainsborough	*Thomas Gainsborough*	74
Gladstone	*William Ewart Gladstone*	76
Gunn Lake	*Donald Gunn*	79
Hargrave Lake	*Joseph James Hargrave*	82
Harte	*[Francis] Bret Harte*	85
Heming Lake	*Arthur Heming*	87
Herchmer	*Lawrence Herchmer*	89
Hudson Bay	*Henry Hudson*	92
Hugo	*Victor Hugo*	94
Ingelow	*Jean Ingelow*	97
Justice	*Mary Jane Holmes*	99
Kelsey	*Henry Kelsey*	102
Knox	*John Knox*	105
Kulish	*Panteleimon Kulish*	108
Landseer	*Edwin Henry Landseer*	110
Munk	*Jens Eriksen Munk (Munck)*	112
Oberon	*William Shakespeare*	114
Ogilvie	*William Ogilvie*	118
Pendennis	*William Makepeace Thackeray*	120
Rembrant	*Rembrandt Harmensz van Rijn*	124

Rennie *John Rennie*	126
Riel *Louis Riel*	128
Rudyard *Rudyard Kipling*	137
St. Boniface *St. Boniface*	141
Sarto *Andrea del Sarto*	143
Selkirk *Thomas Douglas Selkirk*	145
Shelley *Percy Bysshe Shelley*	147
Stonewall *Thomas Jonathan "Stonewall" Jackson*	151
St. Vital *Vital-Justin Grandin*	153
Telford *Thomas Telford*	155
Tipperary *The Song*	157
Tolstoi *Leo Tolstoy*	159
Tremandan *Auguste-Henri de Trémandan*	162
Tyndall *John Tyndall*	164
Tyrrell *Joseph Burr Tyrrell*	167
Wallace Lake *Robert Charles Wallace*	169
Willard *Frances Willard*	171
MANITOBA ABUNDANT AND BEAUTIFUL	173
SOURCES OF MANITOBA PLACE NAMES	174
Churches and Missionaries	174
Explorers and Seamen	175
Fur Trade	175
Royalty	175
Women	176
Politicians	176
Surveyors	177

Aboriginal Names	178
Cree	178
Chippewa	179
Ojibway	179
Assiniboine	179
Sioux	179
MANITOBA AND COUNTING	179
WHILE YOU ARE IN MANITOBA	180
THERE'S MORE IN MANITOBA	183
AFTER THE VIOLENCE	188
SELECTED BIBLIOGRAPHY	194
MAP 1 OF MANITOBA	196
MAP 2 OF MANITOBA	197

Part I

Manitopens

Agassiz

Readers might accept Agassiz Provincial Forest east of Winnipeg as a Manitoba "place name." The individual after whom the area was named was a giant in the field of science.

Louis Agassiz (1807 - 1873)

The Swiss-American geologist, zoologist, and "Father of Glaciology," was born in the French-speaking area of Switzerland and educated in universities in both his home country and Germany as a physician, like many naturalists of the time.

In Paris, Agassiz fell under the tutelage of Alexander Von Humboldt and Georges Cuvier, who helped him on the road to success in zoology and geology. Later, Agassiz served as professor at the Lyceum in Neuchatel, Switzerland. By 1836, he began the study of glaciers as something of a sideline. He integrated the facts to formulate his theory that a great ice age once covered much of the earth. His book *Système Glaciare* (1877) added more information. He believed that Switzerland had once been another Greenland.

Agassiz came to the USA in 1846, and two years later he became a professor at Harvard University, where he began acquiring funding for a great museum of natural history. He and others formed the National Academy of Sciences.

Rather than accepting Darwin's views expressed in his famous "The Origin of Species," Agassiz saw the divine plan of God everywhere in nature. He defined a species as "a thought of God"; in his *Essay on Classification*, he wrote:

> In one word, all these facts in their natural connection proclaim aloud One God, whom man may know, adore and love; and Natural History must in good time become the analysis of the thought of the Creator of The Universe.

Agassiz advanced Cuvier's catastrophism theory: that the earth had periodically been wracked by global catastrophes, after each of which new species of plants and animals had appeared. He "replaced" the Biblical flood with his glaciers, which he called "God's great plough." Glaciers were his last catastrophe. He tried unsuccessfully to find evidence of glaciation in Brazil (where he earlier studied the fish of the area).

It appears that Agassiz brought science to the "men and women in the street" as no one else had before.[1] By the time of his death, he was recognized as America's leading scientist.

Agassiz, the last prominent zoologist to resist Charles Darwin's theories on evolution, died in Cambridge, and was buried at Mount Auburn Cemetery, Massachusetts. A boulder from his home area of Switzerland is his grave's monument. Pine trees from the glacier area in Switzerland (he once had a hut built on the ice) were planted nearby.

Mountains in Utah, California, and Arizona are named in honor of Agassiz. So are craters on the moon, and on Mars. An ancient lake (see map) in North America was also named for him.

Thoughts from Louis Agassiz

-I cannot afford to waste my time making money.

-I will frankly tell you that my experience in prolonged scientific investigations convinces me that a belief in God – a God who is behind and within the chaos of vanishing points of human knowledge – adds a wonderful stimulus to the man who attempts to penetrate into the regions of the unknown.

-I have devoted my whole life to the study of Nature, and yet a single sentence may express all that I have done. I have shown that there is a correspondence between the succession of Fishes in geological times and the different states of their growth in the egg – that is all. It chanced to be a result that was found to apply to other groups, and has led to other conclusions of a like nature.

-The combination in time and space of all these thoughtful conceptions exhibits not only thought, it shows also premeditation, power, wisdom, greatness, prescience, omniscience, providence.

-Classification seems to me to rest upon too narrow a foundation when it is chiefly based on structure. Animals are linked together as closely by their mode of development, by their relative standing in their respective classes, by the order in which they have made their appearance upon earth, by their geographical distribution, and generally by their connection with the world in which they live, as by their anatomy. All these relations should, therefore, be fully expressed in a natural classification; and through structure furnishes the most direct indication of some of these relations, always appreciable under every circumstance, other considerations should not be neglected which may complete our insight into the general plan of creation.

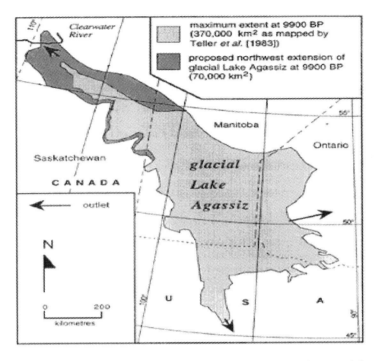

Lake Agassiz was over 1100 km wide and roughly 1500 km long with a depth of 210 meters. The lake's size and depth changed from one age to another. Drainage systems also changed. Lake Agassiz, formed over 11,500 years ago, was the largest glacial lake in North America. Lake Winnipeg and other lakes are remnants of that ancient lake. Continued deglaciation shifted the drainage in to Hudson Bay.

---

1 Another famous scientist, Guglielmo Marconi (1874 - 1937), should be noted here. Marconi, a station located in East Kildonan, is named in his honor. The Italian physicist shared a 1909 Nobel prize for his part in the development of wireless telegraphy. On December 1, 1901, at St. John's Newfoundland, Marconi succeeded in receiving signals transmitted across the Atlantic ocean from Poldhu, Cornwall, England; his success came in spite of the skeptics who believed that the earth's curvature would limit the communication of electric waves

Map: www.und.nodak.edu/instruct/eng/fkarner/picts/agassiz.gif
Photo: www.geraldmassey.org.uk/miller/images/louis_agassiz.jpg

Allegra, Ponemah and Nokomis Lake

Allegra, a post office site east of Selkirk, owes its name to the busy pen of Henry Wadsworth Longfellow. Nokomis Lake, north and a bit east of Grass River Provincial Park, and the Ponemah community near Selkirk also "connect" with the famous author. When you visit these districts, watch for a talented long fellow.

Henry Wadsworth Longfellow (1807 - 1882)

Longfellow, the most popular American poet of the 19th Century, graduated from Maine's Bodoin College in 1825. He then traveled extensively in Europe, and returned to his home college in 1829 as a librarian and professor. His later professorship in Harvard allowed him research time in Heidelberg, Germany, were he was deeply influenced by German romanticism.

After his return to Harvard, he published widely, including *Evangeline* (1847), a highly popular idyll of the former French colony of Acadia (Nova Scotia and neighboring areas). He left university work in 1854, and a year later he published *Hiawatha (Laughing Waters)*, a long narrative poem noted for its use of trochaic meter. He wrongly "placed" Hiawatha too far west (in fact, the chief of the Onondaga tribe lived well to the east). However, among many of his other poems, that work has remained popular up to the present day.

Longfellow's Hiawatha is an Ojibwa Indian raised by Nokomis, his wise old grandmother. The mature Hiawatha wants to avenge the wrong done by the West Wind, his father, who had hurt the youth's mother. Eventually, the son and father reconcile.

Hiawatha becomes leader of his people, and he marries Minnehaha of the former enemy Dakota tribe. Under Hiawatha's leadership, an era of learning and peace takes place.

However, famine and disease later strike the people. Many people, including Hiawatha, die as a result. Before his death, he tells his people to heed those who will come with a new religion. Then, according to the Longfellow poem, the great chief left for the Isles of the Blessed: the kingdom of Ponemah in the Land of the Hereafter.

Perhaps the best known lines from the poem *Hiawatha* are as follows:

> By the shores of Gitche Gumee,
> By the shining Big-Sea Water,
> Stood the wigwam of Nokomis,
> Daughter of the Moon, Nokomis.

The singsong meter of the poem has led to many parodies, some cruel, and many in bad taste. Yes, Longfellow had his opponents. Consider what American critic Van Wyck Brooks says: "Longfellow is to poetry what the barrel-organ is to music."

However, Longfellow's Hiawatha, Minnehaha, and Nokomis have the last word. They have become part of our language and storytelling. Some of his comments follow here:

-Art signifies no more than this. Art is power.

-Art is the revelation of man; and not merely that, but likewise the revelation of nature, speaking through man.

-A boy's will is the wind's will.

-Were half the power that fills the world with terror,
Were half the wealth bestowed on camps and courts,
Given to redeem the human mind from error,
There were no need for arsenals or forts.

-A life that is worth writing at all, is worth writing minutely and truthfully.

-It has done me good to be somewhat parched by the heat and drenched by the rain of life.

-This world loves a spice of wickedness.

-Whenever nature leaves a hole in a person's mind, she generally plasters it over with a thick coat of self-deceit.

-Lives of great men all remind
We can make our lives sublime,
And, departing, leave behind us,
Footprints in the sands of time.

-The cares that infest the day
Shall fold their tents, like the Arabs,
And as silently steal away.

-Sorrow and silence are strong, and patient endurance is godlike. (*Evangeline*)

-Between the dark and the daylight,
When the night is beginning to lower,
Comes a pause in the day's occupations,
That is known as the Children's Hour.

(One of the characters in the Children's Hour was called Laughing Allegra, after whom Allegra, Manitoba was named.)

AMI ISLAND

Pilot your boat north from Birch Island on Lake Winnipegosis and pull ashore on Ami Island, where you might be inspired to study geological formations just as was the man after whom the small island was named.

HENRI-MARC AMI (1858 - 1931)

Dr. Ami was born in Belle-Rivière, Quebec. Son of a Swiss pastor, young Henri studied science at McGill University, where he was inspired by Professor John William Dawson, among others.

In 1882, Ami joined the Geological Survey of Canada, which he served in until 1911. He became well known for his work on geological formations in Quebec and the Maritimes. (His bibliography today contains over 200 titles.) He was editor of the *Ottawa Naturalist,* 1895 - 1900. He was then elected to the RSC (1900). In 1905, he was honored by receiving the Bigsby Medal from the Geological Society of London.

Ami's marriage to Clarissa Burland, whose Montreal family was well-to-do, allowed him freedom from financial worries. So, after his 1911 "retirement", he devoted himself to archaeology, conducting several excavations in southern France. (Many of his findings are housed in the Canadian Museum of Civilization, and in some Canadian universities.)

After his move to France, Ami founded the École Canadienne de Préhistoire, an institution funded by the RSC and the French government. Earlier, he served as curator of geology and paleontology in the National Museum of Canada.

Ami proudly proclaimed in 1915 that "a French Canadian will accomplish as much with an axe as a man of any other race with a full set of tools."

Photo of Henri-Marc Ami taken by William Topley in October, 1897. Library and Archives of Canada, E74403 (Negative E00205157).

Back

The railway point called Back, south of Churchill, is named in honor of a multi-talented individual knighted by the young Queen Victoria.

George Back (1796 - 1878)

This Arctic explorer, naval officer, and artist was not only knighted, but also received the medal of the Royal Geography Society. In 1818, the English-born Back made his first voyage to the Arctic, which captured his imagination. He spent much of his life exploring the Arctic.

While the naval officer was stationed in Halifax, he was chosen to accompany Lt. John Franklin (see *Franklin*) to the Coppermine River region in 1819. There, Back proved to be a hero when he saved comrades' lives during the expedition. In 1824, he joined Franklin overland to Great Bear Lake and the Arctic coast.

On an 1834 search mission for John Ross, he found the Thiew-ee-choh River, now named in Back's honor. (The river flows into Lake Franklin near the Arctic coast.) Honors followed such accomplishments.

However, it is Back the artist that allows him to be called a Manitopen. It seems that he learned water color techniques while a prisoner of war in France (1809-1814). He sketched and painted rock formations, forest fires, campsites, and native life while he traveled the Arctic regions. His talent as a topographer was considerable. Much of this work is preserved in the National Archives of Canada.

View of the Arctic Sea, from the Mouth of the Copper Mine River. Midnight, July 20, 1821. Library and Archives Canada, Acc. No 1970-188-55, W.H. Coverdale Collection of Canadiana

Baden, Powell, and Mafeking

A boy scout with the correct badge will direct you to the area north of Swan River, where three settlements are named in honor of Lord Baden-Powell, founder of the Boy Scouts and military leader.

Lord Baden-Powell (1857 - 1941)

Baden-Powell of Gilwell, Robert Stephenson Smyth Baden-Powell, 1st Baron, belongs with other Manitopens, because in 1908 he published *Scouting for Boys*, a book read and followed by countless thousands of Boy Scouts across the globe. The founder of the Boy Scouts also founded the Wolf Cubs in 1916, and was named World Chief Scout in 1920. With his sister Agnes (1838 - 1945), he also founded the Girl Guides in 1910. The Boy Scout motto: "Be Prepared."

The London-born leader was educated at the famous Charterhouse school. In 1876, he joined the army, served in India, and Afghanistan and Matabeleland in southern Africa. He won fame as the defender of Mafeking during the Boer War (1899-1902). (Ladysmith, a railway point southwest of Portage la Prairie, was also named after a Boer War battle.) In 1907, he was promoted to Lieutenant General.

BEGG LAKE

Begg Lake, a bit east of Thompson, is another Manitoba place name that honors a historian-journalist of the province. His pen and his talents were put to good use.

ALEXANDER BEGG (1840-1897)

Yes, the Quebec-born Alexander Begg had a significant impact on late 19th century Manitoba and beyond. Educated at St. John's, Canada East, and Aberdeen, Scotland, he moved back to Canada. He married Katherine Hamilton, with whom he had two children.

Begg returned to Quebec to a career in business. In 1867, the young man moved to Red River, where he served as agent for several eastern firms. Soon, he was known as a successful trader of manufactured goods. He returned briefly to the east with orders amounting to $90 000. He remained in business in Winnipeg until 1877.

Before working for the Manitoba government as Queen's Printer, Deputy Treasurer, and Auditor, Begg put his pen to work as a journalist. From 1872 to 1874, he published the *Manitoba Trade Review* and the *Gazette and Trade Review*. In 1873 he became editor of the *Daily Nor'Wester,* and in 1877 of the *Daily Herald.*

From 1877 to 1888, Begg was Immigration Agent for the CPR in London, England. He returned to journalism in Seattle, and later in Victoria, where he edited the *Victoria Daily News*.

The busy Begg wrote *The Creation of Manitoba* (1871), *Ten Years in Winnipeg* (1879), *The Great North-West* (1881), and *History of the North-West* (1894-95), among other selections.

The Red River historian clearly merits the accolade Manitopen. After all, he had firsthand knowledge of the Riel Rebellion and the birth of the province.

BELCHER

South of Churchill, the railway point called Belcher is named in honor of a man whose 19th century travels took him to some very dangerous corners of our earth.

EDWARD BELCHER (1799-1877)

Admiral Sir Edward Belcher of the British Royal Navy was born to a prominent political family in Halifax, Nova Scotia. At age thirteen, he enlisted as a first class volunteer in the British Royal Navy. His country was at war.

In 1816, Belcher took part in the Battle of Algiers, in which there was an attempt to suppress Barbary piracy. Two years later, he was promoted to lieutenant. Over the years, he became an explorer, war hero, surveyor, scientist, and a prodigious writer. He authored the classic work *A Treatise on Nautical Surveying* (1835), and his later *Hints to Travelers* included a description of navigational instruments. He also wrote numerous articles for scientific journals.

As a surveyor, Belcher participated in major British naval expeditions to northern Canada, Alaska, Africa, Hawaii, the Far East, United States, Mexico, South America, and the Mediterranean area. In 1829, he was named Commander in the navy. He wrote a two-volume work describing his voyage around the world.

During the Opium War, Belcher played a very active part in the British acquisition of Hong Kong, the capture of Canton, and the cannonading of Chinese forts. Some observers commented on his gallantry and courage. Upon his return to England in 1843, he was honored with a knighthood (he also received a second knighthood in 1867).

In 1852, Captain Belcher was given the difficult task of searching the Canadian Arctic for Sir John Franklin and his crew. (See Franklin). He spent two years in command of the five vessels involved. He did not find Franklin, but he did study and write abut Arctic wildlife, climate, and geography.

In 1872, Belcher was promoted to the rank of Admiral. Two years earlier his wife, Lady Diana, published *Mutineers of the Bounty* describing the famous mutiny on the HMS Bounty.

Today, some writers describe Belcher as a self-serving, vindictive and quarrelsome leader who treated his men badly (little proof is included). Other writers refer warmly to his wisdom, mercy, generosity, intelligence, and compassion. The argument continues.

One wonders why Belcher, explorer and man-of-the-pen, is not as well known as are some lesser explorers, in terms of accomplishments.

It is of interest that the official desk of the President of the United States was made from material taken from the British ship Resolute. In 1852, it was one of the ships commanded by Edward Belcher during his voyage to the Canadian Arctic.

Belcher Islands are located in the southeastern part of Hudson Bay.

Painting of Sir Edward Belcher by Stephen Pearce, National Portrait Gallery, London

BENITO

Southwest of Swan River, a stone's throw from the border with Saskatchewan, is the settlement called Benito, likely named in honor of a character called Benito Cereno, created by the American poet and novelist, Herman Melville.

HERMAN MELVILLE (1819-1891)

Melville's short story *Benito Cereno* is a rich Gothic tale of black revenge and white masters of the slave trade. The racist Yankee Captain Delano went to the aid of a drifting slave ship off the coast of Peru in 1799. Delano wrongly believed that the erratic Captain Benito Cereno and his black servant Babo were guilty of piracy. In fact, the slaves had rebelled, enslaving Cereno and others. Cereno and Delano escaped, but Cereno later died. Recaptured slaves were executed.

Such a story set on the high seas might be expected of Melville, given his own adventures in the South Seas. The New York-born youth shipped out as a sailor in 1837, after long months of study and reading. Four years later, he sailed around Cape Horn in the whaler "Dolly." Later, he and others were held captive on islands frequented by cannibals. The captives were rescued. He later wrote that "a whaleship was my Yale College and my Harvard."

Melville's experiences led him to write (anonymously) magazine stories such as *Benito Cereno,* among others. Several books followed. Unsuccessful lecture tours followed. It appears that Melville was better known and respected in Britain. Human gullibility bothered him.

When he died, he was virtually forgotten. His genius that created *Moby Dick*, and *The Confidence Man; His Masquerade,* and *Billy Budd, Foretopman*, among other titles, was not recognized for many years.

The complex Melville was not a contented individual. He was long bothered by his permanently weakened eyesight caused by scarlet fever when he was a boy. Melville's oldest son committed suicide in 1867. While visiting Nathaniel Hawthorne in Liverpool in 1836, he remarked, "I have just about made up my mind to be annihilated." Hawthorne spoke of Melville's state of mind: "That Calvinistic sense of innate depravity and original sin from whose visitations, in some shape or other, no deeply thinking mind is always and wholly free."

Perhaps the most famous quote from Melville comes from *Moby Dick*, Ch. 135: "Towards thee I roll, thou all-destroying but unconquering whale . . . from hell's heart I stab at thee."

Other quotes of interest include:

-I have written a wicked book (Moby Dick) and feel as spotless as a lamp.

-Give me Vesuvius for an inkstand. [Often Melville would stumble in his work until late afternoon, and then his pen really went to work.]

The famed psychiatrist Carl Jung has the last word here:

-In general, it is the non-psychological novel that offers the richest opportunities for psychological elucidation. Here the author . . . does not show his characters in a psychological light and thus leaves room for analysis and interpretation, or even invites it by his unprejudiced mode of presentation . . . I would also include Melville's *Moby Dick*, which I consider to be the greatest American novel, in this broad class of writings.

BEULAH

Leave Highway #1 west of Virden and take Highway #83 north to Beulah, named in honor of a novel by Augusta Wilson, one of the first women in North America to earn a large income from her writing.

AUGUSTA JANE EVANS WILSON (1835-1909)

The Georgia-born Evans moved with her slave-holding parents to Texas and then to Alabama, where she spent the rest of her life. Augusta had little formal education, but her mother taught her at home and encouraged the girl's intellectual pursuits. Her family was short of money, so the young lady began her writing as her way to add to the family's income.

Wilson's second novel, *Beulah*, was well received by critics and sold well. In that book, as in her other works, her Christian faith was a strong influence. She often featured virtuous heroines who educated themselves before accepting their roles as Christian wives.

However, her love for a Northern journalist who admired Lincoln was not as strong as her love for the Confederate side in the American Civil War (1861-65). She broke off her engagement as a result. She married Lorenzo Wilson, a widower with four children. During the war, she nursed Confederate soldiers. In her novel *Macaria*, she idealized the sacrifices of southern women. Other books followed. One of them, *St. Elmo*, was very popular and sold well. Women's intellectual development was a constant theme in her work. She became a national celebrity.

Augusta Wilson is buried in Mobile's Magnolia Cemetery amid the graves of Confederate soldiers. Fellow novelist Mary Virginia Terhune claimed that "*Beulah* is the best work of fiction ever published by a southern writer."

Bonnie Doon

Take Highway #6 northeast from Winnipeg. Stop at St. Laurent, and secure directions to the nearby Bonnie Doon community. Please adjust your kilt and tune your bagpipe before your arrival. The enclosed words and music might be of help to you.

Robert Burns (1759-1796)

Burns was one of seven children born to a cotter near Alloway, Scotland. Their father moved from one unprofitable farm to another, but he made sure his children were well educated. Young Robert was given a solid grounding in English, including Shakespeare, and much more. The boy was a voracious reader, and while in school he wrote verses for a "hobby." However, Robert's "spare" time was spent as a ploughman and laborer on various farms.

Young Robert experienced poverty, hard work, and injustice, which later increased his belief in the equality of men.

As Burns matured, his writing increased. However, his poverty also continued, so he seriously considered moving to Jamaica. In 1786, his *Poems, Chiefly on the Scottish Dialect* was published, and became a great success. The aristocrats and literary society of Edinburgh embraced him. His fine appearance, gregarious nature, and wit added to his popularity. He became a very serious drinker, as well.

Burns eventually married Jean Armour, but not before he bedded many a Scot lass (some claim that Burns fathered at least fifteen children). His actions led to "a life of dissipation and amorous complexity."[1]

Burns wrote in splendid 18th century English, as well as his native Scots language. His poems owe much to the songs of Scotland. He collected, amended, and wrote over 200 songs such as *Auld Lang Syne, Ye Banks and Braes, O My Love's Like a Red, Red Rose*, among others.

In 1791, Robert Burns published his last major poem, *Tam O'Shanter*.

In 1796, rheumatic heart disease claimed the life of Robert Burns, who is now buried in a Dumfries cemetery. Today, millions of people celebrate his birthday on January 25th: Burns' Night.

Some memorable quotes from Burns include:

-Auld Scotland has a rauche tongue.

-Freedom and whisky gang thegither.

-Should auld acquaintance be forgot
and never brought to mind.

-A fond kiss, and then we sever;
Ae foreword, and then forever.

-Gin a body meet a body
Coming' thro' the rye...

-The healsome porritch, chief of Scotia's food

-An atheist-laugh's a poor exchange
For Deity offended.

-A man's a man for a' that

-Man's inhumanity to man
Makes countless thousands mourn.

-Go fetch to me a pint o' wine,
An' fill it in a silver tassie.

-I'm truly sorry Man's dominion
Has broken Nature's social union.

-Some have meat and cannot eat,
Some can not eat that want it;
But we have meat and we can eat,
Sae let the Lord be thankit.

-Thou eunuch of language, thou pimp of gender,
murderous accoucheur of infant learning,
thou pickle-herring in the puppet show nonsense.
(Note to a critic)

---

1 Margaret Drabble, Ed. *The Oxford Companion to English Literature*. Oxford: Oxford University Press, 2000

YE BANKS AND BRAES.
Solo or Duet.

Words by BURNS. Air, "The Caledonian Hunt's Delight."

Oft hae I rov'd by bonnie Doon,
 To see the rose and woodbine twine;
And ilka bird sang o' its love,
 And fondly sae did I o' mine.
Wi' lightsome heart I pu'd a rose,
 Fu' sweet upon its thorny tree;
And my fause lover stole my rose,
 But ah! he left the thorn wi' me.

BRADWARDINE

A bit northwest of Brandon is the settlement of Bradwardine, named after a character found in Sir Walter Scott's novel *Waverley*. Will you find then "a sneaking piece of imbecility," as Scott described the "original" Waverley?

WALTER SCOTT (1771-1832)

Many experts consider Walter Scott to be the inventor and greatest practitioner of the historical novel. The son of an Edinburgh lawyer suffered from infantile paralysis as a child, and was sent to the country, where he was cared for by an aunt. She told him romantic tales, and read to him from the stirring ballads and legends of the Border Wars. When Scott was a little older, he wandered the border areas, learning the legends as told by the peasants he met. Those stories inspired his later writing. Scott attended the University of Edinburgh, studied law, became a sheriff, but continued to be a voracious reader of history, drama, poetry, romances, and fairy tales.

It was not until he was forty-three years old that he began his career as a novelist. After that, much of his work was done to get rid of his debts. He spent his fortune – and the labors of his last years, often in pain – clearing up those obligations. He died peacefully, but lamented and admired. "The prince of romances" conquered the world with his historical novels. In addition, he has been called "the sweetest singing poet."

Waverley, Scott's first novel, was published in 1814, after his earlier "renditions" were thrown away some years before. The novel's Edward Waverley was a romantic young man who served in the army in Scotland, where he became enmeshed in political and military intrigues. He was rescued by one Rose Bradwardine (after whom the Manitoba settlement was named). Scott claimed that he wrote *Waverley* "without much skill", and in haste. However, many experts consider it to be one of the best plotted of all his works.

The generous, kindly, lover-of-all-mankind is perhaps better known for his 1820 *Ivanhoe*, which treats England in the Age of Richard Coeur-de-Lion. That year, he was made a baronet. His literary conquest had brought Scott wealth and world fame such as no writer before him had enjoyed. The story teller was a master of dialogue.

There is a famous account of Walter Scott and Lady Scott, who passed a field of playful lambs. "No wonder that poets from the past have made lambs the symbols of peace and innocence," noted the writer. His wife replied, "Delightful creatures indeed, especially with mint sauce."

Scott, however, often had the last word. When William Wordsworth said that he had great contempt for Aristotle, Scott responded: "But not, I take it, that contempt which familiarity breeds."

The writer showed wit and quick thinking, even as a boy in school. There, he noted that his debating opponent often fumbled and fiddled with a particular vest button while talking. Secretly, Scott took a pair of scissors and snipped off the boy's button. During the forthcoming debate, his opponent reached for the button, became upset, stuttered, and then fell silent. A victory for young Scott.

In spite of Scott's successes, the British essayist William Nazlett commented: "Sir Walter Scott (when all is said and done) is an inspired butler."

Nearly 100 years after Scott's death, the British novelist E.M. Forster wrote a scathing critique on Scott and his work:

> For my own part I do not care for him, and find it difficult to understand his continued reputation . . . when we fish him out of the river of time . . . he is seen to have a trivial mind and a heavy style. He cannot construct. He has neither artistic detachment, nor passion . . . He only has a temperate heart and gentlemanly feelings, and an intelligent attraction for the countryside, and this is not basis for great novels.

In spite of such criticisms, many of Scott's comments endure. Consider:

-Too many flowers . . . too little fruit (on a fellow writer)

-And come he slow, or come he fast,
It is but Death who comes at last.

-Breathes there the man, with soul so dead,
Who never to himself hath said,
This is my own, my native land.

-Steady of heart, and stout of hand.

-November's sky is chill and drear,
November's leaf is red and sear.

-To lead but one measure, drink one cup of wine.

-The ancient and now forgotten pastime of high jinks.

-'Pax vobiscum' will answer all queries.

-Fair, fat and forty.

-The blockheads talk of my being like Shakespeare - not fit to tie his brogues.

-For love will still be lord of all.

-O what a tangled web we weave,
When first we practice to deceive.

-Music is the universal language of mankind.

Button

What a tremendous story can be triggered by a visit to Button, a railway point approximately half-way between The Pas and Thompson. The story suggests that Manitoba was discovered by accident.

Thomas Button (c. 1570-1634)

Thomas Button, born in Worleton, Wales, saw his first naval service by 1589, and when the Spanish fleet invaded Ireland in 1601, he was captain of the pinnace *Moon*. Because he served with distinction, he won official commendation and a lifetime pension of six shillings eight pence. The following year, he commanded a privateer, the *Wylloby*, in the West Indies.

Some people don't realize that Button, Royal Navy officer and explorer, was the first to fly England's flag over what is now Manitoba. Indeed, it can be said that Button accidentally discovered Manitoba. In 1612, Button and crew sailed from England in two ships, *Resolution* and *Discovery*, with two goals: locate Henry Hudson and other victims of a mutiny (see Hudson Bay), and to further explore the Northwest Passage to the Orient.

The expedition entered Hudson Strait, where Button named Resolution Island for his own vessel. He also named Mansel Island after a friend, on the way to the great Hudson Bay. The ships sailed southwest and down the coast to the large estuary of the Nelson River, then named by Button in honor of Francis Nelson, his sailing master who, among many other crew members, had died of scurvy. They followed the river inland for a short distance, where the ships were trimmed and made ready for what was to be a horrid winter. Button named the west coast of the bay New North Wales and New South Wales, names that faded in time.

The next year, Button headed north in search of the Northwest Passage. The *Resolution* was lost in the ice, but the *Discovery* continued on to 65° North. He had learned that the Hudson Bay was a wide land-locked sea, and he found no trace of Hudson.

After his return to England in 1613, his success was assured. He became an admiral, and was knighted in 1616 (this was the same individual who had appeared before magistrates sixteen years earlier on a charge of robbing the home of a widow. Influential people applied pressure, and the young man was set free.) The vigorous Button served as rear admiral in the 1620-21 campaign against the pirates along the cost of Algeria.

But why might Thomas Button be called a Manitopen? Yes, his navigational skills would require a pen (quill), but there is also another reason: During his search for the Northwest Passage, he carried letters of introduction to the Orient, or "the Land of Silk and Spices." He later offered to take the journal of his voyage to the king.

Nearly 400 years later, there are now claims that some of those "water routes", i.e., Northwest Passage, don't belong to Canada alone. What would Button say about that?

For many years, Hudson Bay was called Button Bay. The courageous and able Button was made Admiral of the Irish coast.

Relevant Comments:

-Button was a well-connected . . . and high-spirited man and had no pedantic attachment to the niceties of the law.
George Malcolm Thomson, *The North-West Passage*, London, Futura Publ. Ltd., 1975, p. 85.

-Observe well the flood. If it aim to South-west, you may be sure the [Northwest] Passage is that way.
Henry, Prince of Wales, to Thomas Button, 1612.

-For we assure ourself by God's grace you will not return [to England], without either the good news of a Passage or sufficient assurance of an impossibility.
Henry, Prince of Wales, to Thomas Button, 1612.

-They of Canada say that it is a month's space to saile to a lande where cinnamon and cloves are growing.
Divers Journeys, London, 1582.

-I wish that some learned man would write of [scurvy] for it is the plague of the sea and the spoil of mariners.
Richard Hawkins, 1622.

-The captains [for the Northwest discovery] must be skilful and good cosmographers, men of good reputation and of great solution . . . to perform such a voyage . . . [and] their commission must give them liberty to punish with death if mutinies or disorders arise.
Sir William Monson, sailor with Button, among others.

-The said islands [the goal of Button, among others] abound in Gold, Rubies, Diamonds, Bolasses, Granates, Jacinots, and other stones and pearls.
Robert Thorne to Sir Edward Lee, ambassador of King Henry VIII (1491-1547).

-I do confidently believe there to be a [Northwest] Passage as there is one between Calais and Dover.
Thomas Button.

BYLOT

Twenty-five kilometers or so south of Churchill is Bylot, a railway point named after Robert Bylot, sailor, mutineer(?), navigator, explorer. If you are able, fly to the Arctic Island also named for him.

ROBERT BYLOT (CA. 1610)

Bylot was one of the most daring of the early explorers of Canada's north. He was the mate on Henry Hudson's ship, *Discovery*, which sailed into the Hudson Bay in 1611. The strife, fear, and distress on board led some crew members to set Hudson and his son – plus seven other sailors – adrift in an open boat (some people doubt that Bylot was involved in the mutiny). Those nine people were never again seen. The mutiny is a sad chapter in Canadian history.

It seems clear that the *Discovery* would not have made it back to England without the fine navigational skills of Bylot. English authorities recognized that point, and gave Bylot a pardon for any role he had in the mutiny:

> As soon as they arrived [back] in London, Bylot and Abacuck Prickett . . . told . . . their sorrowful tale of mutiny, famine and death. Twenty-two had sailed and only eight returned. Four men had been killed fighting with the Eskimos. One had died of hunger. Nine [including Hudson and his twelve-year-old son] had been deliberately left by their shipmates.[1]

With Thomas Button, he returned to Hudson Bay in 1612. They reached the mouth of the Nelson River and then sailed north to latitude 65° before returning home.

The dogged Bylot was determined to find the Northwest Passage to the Orient. In 1615-16, Bylot and crew made those attempts. However, they learned that the Hudson Bay did not solve their problem.

Perhaps Bylot's "navigational pen" was not as sharp as that of William Baffin, after whom Canada's largest island is named. Baffin and Bylot traveled through many of the straits between the Arctic islands, but they failed to find the passage to the Orient. They reached 77° North latitude, a record that lasted well over 225 years.

After Bylot returned to England, he faded into obscurity. It appears that the Hudson mutiny was the cause. Bylot Island is off the north shore of Baffin Island.

---

1 George Malcolm Thomson. *The North-West Passage*. London: Futura Publications, 1975, p. 82.

Cabot

Travel a bit west of Winnipeg, and you will find the railway point called Cabot, named in honor of the discoverer of North America.

John Cabot (c. 1449-1498)

John (Giovanni) Cabot (Caboto), the Anglo-Italian explorer and navigator, made his two voyages from Bristol, England, to North America in 1497 and 1498. His birthplace was likely Genoa, Italy, but around 1461 he moved to Venice. In 1495, he migrated to England.

Some experts claim that Cabot, "a most expert mariner and map-maker and globe-maker" (the Asian continent bulged into the Atlantic Ocean), was familiar with Marco Polo's account of the far east. Cabot's reading of Polo might well have led him to discount Columbus's claim that he had reached Cathay (China). Therefore, Cabot believed that the western sea route to Asia remained to be discovered. He earlier visited Arabia.

Cabot's 1497 landing in North America was the first known landing there since the Vikings made theirs nearly 500 years earlier. In 1496, King Henry VII authorized Cabot and his three sons to search for the unknown lands to the west. Their ship, the *Matthew*, left Bristol in May 1497, and they landed in North America thirty-five days later, perhaps in Newfoundland, Cape Breton Island, or Labrador. The king's orders: "to discover and find whatever isles, countries, regions or provinces of heathens, in whatsoever part of the world they be, which before this time were unknown to all Christians."[1] When Cabot made his brief North American landing, he met with no other human beings.

By August, Cabot was back in Bristol with his Venetian wife and his sons. His discoveries and his accounts of the tremendous supply of Grand Banks' fish brought him considerable praise. The king awarded "the Conqueror of the New World" a payment of £10 "to hym that found the new Isle." Cabot was called "the Great Admiral", and "he goes dressed in silk, and these English run after him like mad." He made a world map and a globe showing where he had travelled. Copies of the map appeared in other European cities.

In February 1498, royal letters patent authorized "John Kaboto, Venetian" to take "ships of 200 tons or smaller burden, to conduct them to the londe and Iles of late founde by the seid John."[2] Cabot's 1498 journey included five ships and 300 men. They likely landed in Greenland before sailing along Canada's eastern coast. Perhaps they went as far south as Chesapeake Bay.

Cabot perished during his second voyage. The silk-shirted dandy was no more. No one knows what happened. Perhaps one of his ships made it back to Bristol.

His voyages provided the basis for England's claim to North America, and they led to the beginning of the rich North West Atlantic fishing. The navigator-map maker surely deserves to be called a man-of-the-pen.

The Cabot Memorial Tower was constructed in Bristol. The explorer is also remembered by Cabot Trail, in Cape Breton.

Sebastian, John Cabot's son, also became famous for his explorations. The son attempted to find the Northwest Passage.

Other relevant quotes:

-I have "discovered . . . the country of the Grand Khan."
Cabot's claim

-You are to sail "to all parts, countries and seas of the East, of the West, and of the North."
King Henry VII's orders to Cabot.
Note: the order excluded the Spanish-discovered lands of the Caribbean region.

-Cabot intends to travel more and more towards the east (i.e., westward towards East Asia) until he reaches Cipango (Japan).
   Comment by recorder Soneino, regarding Cabot's plans.

-. . . he is believed to have found the new lands nowhere but on the very bottom of the ocean, to which he is thought to have descended together with his boat . . . since after that voyage he was never seen again anywhere[3]
15th century comment on Cabot.

-The codfish were so plentiful "that at times they even stayed (stopped) the ship's passage."
Cabot, referring to the Grand Banks.

---

1 Quoted in R.A. Skelton "John Cabot," "Dictionary of Canadian Biography," Vol. I, p. 148.
2 Ibid.
3 Ibid. p. 151.

Carman

Southwest of Winnipeg at the junction of Highways 3 and 13 you'll find Carman, a center named in honor of a distinguished Canadian clergyman.

Albert Carman (1833-1917)

Albert Carman, born in Iroquois, Upper Canada, attended a school founded by his uncle. Young Albert's bad study habits produced very bad report cards. The boy was described as "the worst of the lot."

However, Carman later "bloomed academically and spiritually," taking his bachelor's and master's degrees from Victoria University, Toronto. He converted to Methodism.

When the Methodist Episcopal Church established Belleville Seminary in 1857, the twenty-three-year-old Carman became a mathematics professor there. A year later, the genial man was named Principal. For two decades, he served as an educator and administrator before becoming a clergyman. He had been severely tempted by the pursuit of wealth, and by the pull of personal pride. Much prayer followed. He decided to live a life controlled by the Holy Spirit and the teachings of Christ.

At age twenty-five, Carman wrote his covenant, in which he promised to devote himself to God: "O Lord help me! You know the motives of the children of men. Make, O make mine right in your sight, for by you I shall be judged and rewarded according to living life here below."[1] Carman felt that God had begun to take possession of his soul.

Albert Carman became fully committed to the personal piety of traditional Methodism. He opposed those Methodists who advocated the higher criticism or scientific study of the Bible. His views allowed him to rise steadily in Methodist leadership circles. He became bishop of the Methodist Episcopal Church before the 1884 union of all Canadian Methodist churches. He served as general superintendent after union until his retirement.

Carman wrote and spoke about the need for "holy living" while insisting on the authority of the Bible. He stressed that alcohol was the source of many social problems. He also successfully encouraged Methodist missions in Manitoba and other parts of Western Canada.

By 1910, the liberals of his church gained more power than the traditionalists or conservatives. The liberal theology, according to Carman, stressed "good works" rather than the teachings of Christ. The pleasant clergyman-administrator had frequent fights with those liberals.

Dr. Albert Carman, one of the greatest leaders of Canadian Methodists, retired in 1914. A bit later, a bad fall broke his hip, an accident from which he never fully recovered. The pious gentleman died in 1917.

On the former site of Tabernacle United Church in Belleville, Ontario, a plaque was placed in honor of Albert Carman:

ALBERT CARMAN 1833 - 1917

A commanding figure in Canadian Methodism during the late 19th and early 20th centuries, Carman was born in Iroquois and educated at Victoria College, Cobourg. He worked briefly as a teacher and was then appointed principal of Belleville Seminary, later Albert College, in 1858. A masterful administrator and, after entering the Methodist Episcopal ministry, a militant advocate for Methodist education, Carman spearheaded the successful development of this Methodist school during his 17-year term there. Following his election as a Bishop in 1874, he gained increasing prominence in church affairs, particularly as an ardent supporter of union among the Methodists denominations. When union was achieved in 1884, Carman became a General Superintendent of the Methodist Church, a post he held until his retirement in 1914.

Erected by the Ontario Heritage Foundation,
Ministry of Culture and Communications

---

1 Albert Carman, Canadian Methodist Holiness Leader" Occasional Paper, Christian History Institute, 2006, Electronic version, p. 2

Cauchon Lake

A short flight east from Thompson will take you to Cauchon Lake, named in honor of a journalist-writer-politician of distinction.

Joseph Édouard Cauchon (1816-1885)

Cauchon, a descendant of one of Quebec's oldest families, was educated at the Petite Séminaire de Quebec, and was called to the bar in 1843. Rather than practicing law, Cauchon's interests turned to journalism and politics.

By 1841, Cauchon was a regular contributor to *Le Canadien*, a leading exponent of French Canadian nationalism. Later he began his *Le Journal de Quebec*, which became a very influential newspaper in that it had an important role in the public debates leading to Confederation.

In 1864-65, Cauchon published a series of articles carefully defending the seventy-two Quebec Resolutions, which were a strong base of eventual Confederation. His belief in a united Canada was expressed in his *L'Union des Provincie de l'Amerique Britannique du Nord*.

Always something of a political maverick, Cauchon served as MLA and MP (Montmorency County), and later as the first Speaker of the Senate after Confederation. From 1877 to 1882, he served with distinction as Lieutenant-Governor of Manitoba. Cauchon earned his reputation as a fiercely partisan politician and journalist.

Image: The Hon. Joseph Édouard Cauchon, P.C.
Source: Library and Archives Canada

Coldwell Lake

Coldwell Lake is a bit north of the sprawling Sipiwash Lake. Fly from Thompson to that smaller lake, named in honor of a pioneer editor-journalist-publisher who played an important role in the formation of Manitoba. Coldwell Creek, which flows into Pikwitonei River, is also named after him.

William Coldwell (1834-1907)

The London-born, Dublin-educated Coldwell came to Canada in 1854. The young man was a correspondent for the *Toronto Leader* until 1859, when he journeyed to Red River with William Buckingham to found the *Nor'Wester*, the first newspaper in what became Manitoba. The publication frequently attacked the establishment of the time: particularly the "privileged charter" of the HBC. Coldwell and his colleagues preached annexation with Canada.

The newspaper office was destroyed by fire in early 1865, and Coldwell returned to Toronto, where he became a reporter for the *Globe*. Four years later, he returned to Red River to found the *Red River Pioneer*. Louis Riel seized the paper for his own use.

Coldwell opposed Riel and his resistance to the "takeover" of the region by Canada. During the rebellion, Coldwell was clerk of the Provisional Assembly. In 1871, he began the publication of the *Manitoban,* which later merged with the *Manitoba Free Press*. Because of bad health, William Coldwell retired in 1877, and died twenty years later in Victoria, British Columbia. Earlier, he had married Jemima Ross, with whom he had four children.

In 1888, Coldwell was invited to attend the reunion banquet of Winnipeg Newspapermen. Because of illness, he could not be present, but he did write the following account which was read at the banquet:

On Nov. 1, 1859, the first newspaper outfit for the Northwest British American arrived at the crossing of the Assiniboine River opposite Upper Fort Garry. Up to that day no newspaper was printed anywhere throughout the vast region stretching from the north shore of Lake Superior to the Rocky Mountains, and from the United States boundary line as far north as anyone of our craft would care to go. In one little corner of the territory was the Red River Settlement and here we resolved to open fire.'

The paper, ink, and much of the plant had been purchased in St. Paul, Minnesota, in order to save freight, and on the 28th of September we made a start with ox teams – a very wild start indeed, as one team ran away at the beginning and distributed much of the type in the streets.

I shall not stop to note our snail-like progress by the Crow Wing Trail, how we struggled through the swamps, worried around and across fallen trees and stumps, toiled up and raced down the sides of the Leaf Mountains, forded rivers with steep banks and boulder-strewn beds, zigzagging along, while occasional incursions into the Red Lake River – the wildest, deepest, crookedest and swiftest in current – took us up to our necks and nearly cost me my life. On the average we did not exceed between 15 and 20 miles a day in our march through the wilderness to the promised land . . .

Here we commenced publication on Dec. 28, 1859, and at the outset were greater monopolists than we had any wish to be. We were our own editors, reporters, compositors, pressmen, newsboys, and general delivery agents. We secured a liberal subscription for our fortnightly paper-payment in advance. The subscription price was 12 shillings (Hudson's Bay Company currency), afterwards reduced to 10 shillings.[1]

Now there was a man-of- the-pen!

---

[1] Quoted in Edith Patterson. *Tales of Early Manitoba*. Winnipeg: The Winnipeg Free Press. 1970, p. 23.
Photo: Arthur P. Coldwell, courtesy of Whyte Archives, V14 ACOOP-82

Coleman Island

Coleman Island and Coleman Bay are in Sagemace Bay, found off the southwest shore of Lake Winnipegosis. Both place names honor a distinguished mountain man, geologist, author, and academic.

Arthur P. Coleman (1852-1939)

University of Toronto geology professor, the La Chute, Quebec-born Arthur Coleman, completed eight exploratory trips in the Canadian Rockies and Selkirks. He was aided by his remarkable brother and outfitter, L. Quincy Coleman.

The professor first visited the mountains of western Canada in 1884, reaching the then end of the railway at Laggan (Lake Louise). He wrote of that experience:

> It was only a commonplace mountain, about eight thousand feet high, without a name, so far as I am aware, but it belonged to the family of Rocky Mountains, and gave one an introduction to its stately neighbors, for here one could gaze up and down the pass with nothing but clean air between one and the summits, while down in the valley a trail of smoke from the "right of way" [CPR construction] where the timber was burning blurred and sullied the view . . . Northward, up Bow River, one could see a blue lake at its source [now known as Hector Lake]; and across the main valley, with its smoke and bustle, rose several fine mountains with glaciers, and at the foot of one of them beautiful Lake Louise.

Coleman continued his journey to Golden and the Selkirks. On his return trip, Coleman paused to climb Castle Mountain. He wrote:

Above the edge of the cliff, however, going was easy, so that the highest part of the Castle (nine thousand feet) was not hard to reach, and the wonderful view of the valley of Bow River, four thousand feet below, was quite worth seeing. The tower standing in front of the Castle to the southeast looked as unscalable as it was reported to be.

Coleman returned to "his" beloved mountains the next year, again in 1888, 1892, and 1893. He relied heavily on natives' knowledge of the trails and mountain passes. In 1902, Coleman focused on Mount Robson, which he unsuccessfully attempted to climb, because of bad weather. Six years later, the same tough weather prevented that climb. The doughty Coleman made his last trip to the Rockies in his eighties.

His interest went far beyond the Rockies. His primary geologic interest was glaciers. He traveled the world gathering data and photographs of glaciers. Coleman painted many mountain scenes. Perhaps his most well known painting is *The Mountain and The Sky,* which displays Mount Robson.

Mount Coleman in the Saskatchewan River valley is named in his honor. His book *The Canadian Rockies, New and Old Trails* tells of his experiences in the mountains of western Canada: a Canadian literary classic.

Coleman received L.L.D.s from Queen's University in 1913, and from the University of Western Ontario in 1922. He also received D.Sc. from the University of Toronto in 1922, a honorary degree from the University of Adelaide, Australia in 1928, and the Victoria Medal from the Royal Geographical Society in 1933.

Fittingly, Mount Quincy near Jasper is named after brother Lucius Quincy Coleman.

Dafoe Lake

Fly your float plane east from Thompson, and enjoy the incredible scene below you. Set your plane down on Dafoe Lake, named after the man often called "the oracle of Winnipeg." Reflect on the life of that remarkable Canadian and genuine Manitopen.

John Wesley Dafoe (1866-1944)

"The huge, rough set figure, the shaggy head of reddish hair, the carved-stone face" described J.W. Dafoe, the oracle of Winnipeg who was "the greatest Canadian of his time [and who] did a large part of Canada's thinking" for nearly fifty years. "The ubiquitous reporter and wisest counselor [and] ablest political thinker" was the voice and heart of the Liberal Party. Those observations were made by the distinguished journalist-author, Bruce Hutchinson.

Born in the Ottawa Valley bush country, Dafoe was raised on Shakespeare, the Bible, and the *Toronto Globe*. Later, he became a reporter in Montreal and then in Ottawa, where he recorded some of John A. Macdonald's speeches. The young journalist later became advisor to and admirer of Prime Minister Wilfred Laurier, whom he described as "a man who had affinities with Machiavelli as well as Sir Galahad." As Hutchinson stated, "for twenty years [Dafoe] watched over the shoulder of Mackenzie King, with a look of general approval but some scepticism." When Conservative Prime Minister Borden went to the 1919 Peace Conference, he took Dafoe with him as advisor and observer. (Dafoe once said of Borden: "A Grit in disguise or [else] I'm a Tory.") Dafoe firmly believed that "the making of peace is in fact more difficult than has been the winning of the war."

As editor of the *Manitoba* – later the *Winnipeg Free Press* – from 1901 until his death, he became one of the most influential journalists in Canadian history. The proud Canadian was read "across the nation." Some observers considered him a lone voice against the growing power of Adolf Hitler. Dafoe was angered by the Munich agreement and the way Mackenzie King initially underestimated the dictator (the Prime Minister called Hitler "a simple sort of peasant") before World War II. After Munich, the irrepressible Dafoe took his stubby pencil and scribbled his most famous editorial, headed *What's the Cheering For?* He knew it was a fake peace. He correctly claimed that Hitler would conquer Europe, threaten democracies everywhere, and drag America into war. Many people disagreed with him.

The rumpled newsman believed that "a Prime Minister under the party system as we have it in Canada is of necessity an egotist and autocrat." Dafoe continued: "If he comes to office without these characteristics his environment equips him with them as surely as a diet of royal jelly transforms a worker into a queen bee." The critic added: "The ego and the country soon become interblended in his mind." The Prime Minister, according to Dafoe, is not merely the first among equals, not just the chief minister. He is the boss. He remains Prime Minister just as long as he wins elections.

On a 1921 voyage to the Commonwealth Conference (of which he was a strong supporter) in Australia, another journalist asked Dafoe (raised in a Conservative family) why he was such a dyed-in-the-wool Grit (Liberal). "Very simple," he responded, "I simply think of all the sons-of-bitches in the Liberal Party, and I can't help coming to the conclusion that there are more sons-of-bitches in the Tory Party." Strong words from a teetotaller!

As a man of the political center, he distrusted the extremes of the left and the right. He wrote several books, including *Laurier: A Study in Canadian Politics,* and *Canada: An American Nation.* "More than any country in the world," he wrote, "Canada is the result of political, not economic forces."

It remains difficult to name a Canadian political writer who has had more influence than John Wesley Dafoe.

A memorable quote from Dafoe: "There are only two kinds of government – the scarcely tolerable and the absolutely unbearable." His pen was sharp: "Politics in its more primitive and vigorous manifestations is not a game of sport, but a form of civil war, with only lethal weapons barred."

The man had his moments of self-deprecation and quiet humor. When he was offered a title he responded: "How could I accept a knighthood? Good heavens! I shovel off my own sidewalk and stoke my own furnace." He had other moments when he wrote:

-Man must know, if he has any capacity for reason, that modern war doesn't come to end . . . and it sets going a process of destruction that goes on year after year in widening circles of damage and violence.

-Men may fail to be heroes to their valets but they are more successful with their biographers.

-It is no part of a newspaper's function to defend a corporation: it is always able to defend itself.

-The British Empire is a partnership of nations of equal status united in a partnership of consent.

-There is no mania quite so self-revealing as that of Jew-baiting.

-Memory is one of the least reliable manifestations of the mind; it is the handmaid of will and desire.

-Unless we can trade with the outside world our condition must be one of stagnation . . .

-The towering skyline of Toronto in the 1930's depends on the miner in the northern ranges of Ontario. The height of one is in balance with the depth of the other.

-Peace with friction for a century (on Confederation)

-Even majorities have rights.

Dand

If the citizens of Dand read (or reread) the poetry of Archibald Lampman, will they change the settlement's name[1] back to the earlier Lampman named in honor of that poet? Dand is a short, pleasant drive north of Deloraine.

Archibald Lampman (1861-1899)

Many experts consider Lampman the finest 19th century Canadian poet. The civil servant (he worked unhappily in the Post Office Department in Ottawa) was known as one of the "Confederation" poets. Born in Canada West's Morpeth, he later obtained a B.A. at Toronto's Trinity College. He had been introduced to poetry by his father, a classical scholar. Young Lampman read the Greek tragic poets in Greek. He admired the English poets Wordsworth, Keats, Arnold, and Milton.

The moody, shy and somewhat reclusive Lampman had a small circle of friends – intellectuals and writers – in Ottawa. On occasion, he read papers and poetry to various scientific and literary groups. Perhaps his sonnets were and are best appreciated. The public learned that the strikingly handsome Lampman was at the height of his power when contemplating and observing nature, where, like Wordsworth, he found spiritual strength.

The young poet's poor health and the death of his young son seem to have led to his spiritual malaise. During one of his many camping trips to the woodlands, he over-strained his heart.

Four years before his death, he was elected Fellow of the Royal Society of Canada. He loved his homeland, but he wrote this lament: "How utterly destitute of all light and charm are the intellectual conditions of our people and the institutions of our public life. How barren! How barbarous!"

However, Lampman also wrote poetry with a positive note. Part of *The Largest Life* is as follows:

There is a beauty at the goal of life,
A beauty growing since the world began,
Through every age and race, through lapse and strife,
Till the great human soul completes her span

Admirers of Lampman's poetry can also enjoy his *Heat, Solitude, Midnight, In November, Winter Evening, The City of the End of Things* (a somber allegory of human life), *The Truth, Among the Millet,* and *The Violinist*, among many others. Life's unfairness is expressed clearly in Lampman's *To a Millionaire*.

Repelled by the mechanization of urban life, Lampman's poetry sensitively records the feelings evoked by the incidents and scenes he found in his beloved outdoors.

With a very sharp pen, Lampman wrote *The Modern Politician*:

What manner of soul is his to whom high truth
Is but the plaything of a feverish hour,
A dangling ladder to the ghost of power!
Gone are the grandeurs of the world's iron youth,
When kings were mighty, being made by swords.

Now comes the transit age, the age of brass,
Blinding the multitude with specious words.
To them faith, kinship, truth and verity
Men's sacred rights are very holiest thing,

Are but the counters at a desperate play,
Flippant and reckless what the end may be,
So that they glitter, each his little day,
The little mimic of a vanquished king.

(Do you know any politician "to whom high truth is but a plaything"?)

With poetry, Lampman honored the heroism of Adam Dollard des Ormeaux who, with seventeen soldiers, saved Ville Marie (later called Montreal) from the Iroquois in 1660. After ten days of fighting near today's Cornwall, all the men were killed or captured. Lampman's *At the Long Sault: May 1660* should be considered a Canadian classic:

> Silent, white-faced, again and again
> Charged and hemmed round by furious hands,
> Each for a moment faces them all and stands
> In his little desperate ring; like a tired bull moose
> Whom scores of sleepless wolves, a ravening pack,
> Have chased all night, all day
> Through snow-laden woods, like famine let loose;
> As he turns at last in his track
> Against a wall of rock and strands at bay;
> Round him with terrible sinews and teeth of steel
> They charge and recharge; but with many a furious plunge and wheel,
> Hither and thither over the trampled snow,
> He tosses them bleeding and torn;
> Till, driven, and ever to and fro
> Harried. Wounded and weary grown,
> His mighty strength gives way
> And all together they fasten upon him and drag him down.

Further Lampman thoughts:

-I love the face of every man whose thought is swift and sweet.

-The frost that stings like fire upon my cheek . . .

- . . . and wintry grief is a forgotten guest.

-Children of Silence and Eternity,

-They know no season but the end of time.

-Of bipeds, all the way down
　To the pimp and the politician.
　I saw the haggard dreadfulness
　Of old age and death.

-When the strength of man is shattered,
　And the powers of earth are scattered,
　From beneath the ghostly ruin
　Peace still rises.

-The happiest man is he who has cultivated to the utmost
　the sense of beauty.

-So wonderful, so many and so near,
　And then the golden moon to light me home –
　The crunching snowshoes and the stinging air,
　And silence, frost and beauty everywhere.

---

1 Lampman is also found in southeastern Saskatchewan. It was named in the poet's honor.

Dennis Lake

Dennis Lake is a large wetland northeast of Inwood, a settlement halfway between the southern ends of Lake Manitoba and Lake Winnipeg. The wetland is named after an individual who had a stumbling role in the birth of Manitoba.

John Stoughton Dennis (1820-1885)

Dennis is remembered as the man who brought the first survey party to Red River in 1869. Many of the local citizens hated the intrusion. The arrival quickly aroused the suspicion of the Métis, who correctly believed that the event meant the loss of their lands. Yes, the arrival of Dennis and his crew led to the insurrection led by Louis Riel in 1869.

Dennis – the Kingston-born soldier-surveyor-civil servant-businessman of United Empire Loyalist stock, educated at Colburg's Victoria College – was, in 1843, commissioned surveyor in the Department of Crown Lands. For some years, he served his profession in Ontario. Loyalty and military virtues were important to him. He joined the militia in 1885, and seven years later he became Brigade Major of No. 3 Military District, Toronto.

In June 1866, Dennis saw action during the Fenian invasion. Following an exchange of fire, he ordered a retreat. The tugboat left without him, and he was forced to disguise himself as a "laboring man." He escaped, but thirty-four of his men did not. Later, fellow soldiers labeled him "a coward and a Poltrooney Scoundrel." The court exonerated Dennis.

In 1869, Dennis was placed in charge of surveying the North-West Territories. As noted earlier, his arrival to Red River helped to precipitate the Riel rebellion-resistance.

Two years later, he and his crew were made responsible for mapping the prairie provinces. He was later named Deputy Minister of the Interim Department.

During his retirement, Dennis maintained his close relationship with his family and his "dear old chief," Sir John A. Macdonald. He also invested in several private business concerns.

An excellent summation of Dennis' career follows:

> Although he may be remembered as a militia officer who was prone to leap upon his horse and ride off in all directions at once, he should also be recalled as an able administrator who made significant, lasting contributions to Canada.[1]

---

1 Colin Frederick Read, "Dennis, John Stoughton," *The Dictionary of Canadian Biography*, Vol XI, p. 246.

Dugas

Fly your small plane south from Thompson and west of Sipiwesk Lake and land on Dugas Lake, named in honor of a controversial writer.

Abbé Georges Dugas (1833-1928)

The Quebec born and educated Georges Dugas was ordained as a Catholic priest. In his early thirties, he moved to Red River, where he served as a missionary. He met and preached to many Métis there, and he became an admirer and defender of their way of life.

Meanwhile, his attitude toward the prairie Indians was a sour one, and very uncomplimentary. He once wrote that Indians "must be ruled by fear just as we tame wild animals by exerting that power."

During the 1869-70 Red River Rebellion (Resistance) Dugas wrote anonymous articles to French newspapers in Quebec defending the Métis point of view. He strongly supported the cause of Louis Riel. It was Dugas who brought the news of Riel's execution to the Riel family.

The day of the execution, the Abbé Dugas, rector of St. Boniface Cathedral, drove in a sleigh to the Riel home in St. Vital. Louis' mother heard the sleigh approach, its runners singing in the crisp snow. She looked out a window. The priest climbed slowly from the sleigh, turned to the house, walked a few steps up the path, and paused. He made the sign of the cross over the house. Julie screamed and fainted.[1]

Father Dugas fully believed that his twenty-two years in the west equipped him to write his seminal history, *The Canadian West: Its Discovery by the Sieur De La Verendrye [and] Its Development by the Fur-Trading Companies, down to the year 1822*.[2] He claimed he read "all the important sources."

The priest-historian stressed two central figures in his book: La Verendrye and Lord Selkirk. For him, they were "the most interesting figures on the historical canvas of the

North-West": one an explorer, and the other, Selkirk, a "colonizer and civilizer of these wild regions." According to Dugas, Lord Selkirk carried "the first seeds of real civilization" by supporting the area's missionaries. He added: "the Catholics of Manitoba owe him an immense debt of gratitude." Dugas was equal in his praise for the explorer, "a man of genius" and courage.

The pen of Dugas also defended Scot Protestants who were "persecuted and columniated by a company [the North West Company] that flaunted the title of a French company."

During his long life, Dugas continued to express his strong support of the Métis. In 1888, he returned to Quebec.

Selected quotations from his book best express his priorities and opinions:

-The adventurous life of the Canadian trapper . . . was perhaps more real than is commonly believed.

-Then it was that God infused into the heart of a noble Canadian [La Verendrye] . . . the heroic resolution of attempting, at his own expense, and at the risk of his future and the future of his family, the discovery of the west.

-The missionary priests . . . largely contributed to the gaining over of the aborigines to the French.

-The Indians long remembered the [early] Frenchmen who had lived amongst them and who had brought the light of civilization to their tribes.

-In the eye of God, [our] permanent plan is the establishment of Holy Church for the salvation of souls and the greater glory of his Divine Son.

-The Indian life had charms for them [voyageurs]. They imagined that out in the wilds, freed from all restraint, dressed in Indian fashion, sleeping with them in wigwams, and hunting for a livelihood, nothing more could be desired.

-The warfare carried on between the two Companies [the HBC and the NWC] in the North-West could not but end in ruins.

-His [Lord Selkirk] reputation as a distinguished man of large and elevated views had already preceded him.

-So, with his rare intelligence, Lord Selkirk saw that the only way to ensure the livelihood of a colony on the banks of the Red River was to secure as large a tract of territory as possible.

-Hundreds and hundreds of our people left their corpses on the wild deserts of the West. Some of them lost on the plains, died of hunger and fatigue, others perished with the cold, and again others were killed by the Indians. Sometimes they lost their lives in obeying the orders of leaders who treated them like slaves.

-The notoriety of the egotist dies with himself.

-Rarely is history impartially written.

---

1 Joseph Kinsey Howard. *Strange Empire: The Story of Louis Riel.* Toronto: Swen Publishing, 1952, pp 471-472.

2 This translation was made in 1905. Dugas wrote his work in French.

Emerson

Follow the Red River south to Manitoba's border with Minnesota and you'll find Emerson, named after a controversial but often-quoted thinker and literary giant. Perhaps a few locals will argue transcendentalism with you.[1]

Ralph Waldo Emerson (1803-1882)

The Boston-born Emerson was the son of a Unitarian minister who came from a famous line of ministers. Ralph's father, who called his son "a rather dull scholar," died when the boy was two weeks short of his eighth birthday. At age fourteen, the youth went to Harvard College, where he "waited at Commons" to save money. During winter vacation, he taught at his uncle's school in Waltham, Massachusetts.

After his 1821 Harvard graduation, Emerson served as schoolmaster for a while before attending Harvard's Divinity School. The then Unitarian minister later disputed with church officials over the administration of the Communion Service. He resigned in 1832. His first wife Ellen Tucker died of tuberculosis the previous year.

In 1832-33, Emerson, essayist and poet, toured Europe; there, he met with a number of literary giants such as Coleridge, Mill, Carlyle, and Wordsworth. Five years later, he visited Italy, France, and the Middle East. He sustained a correspondence with Carlyle until the latter's death in 1881.

After Emerson purchased a home in Concord, Massachusetts, he became a leading citizen of the area. He married Lydia Jackson, with whom he had four children.

In 1833 Emerson and others founded the Transcendental Club, which later published its journal, *The Dial*, which became a major foundation for Transcendentalism. Three years later, he gave his famous Harvard Divinity Address, with which he outraged the Protestant establishment and community by stating that Jesus was a great man, but was not God. His comments led him to be called an atheist and a poisoner of young minds.

Emerson made a decent living as a popular lecturer in New England and beyond. He was known as an abstract and difficult writer, but one who drew large crowds for his speeches. Indeed, he was known as one of the great orators of his time. His energy, deep voice, and egalitarian respect for his audience won him large audiences. Yet Emerson insisted that he wanted no followers, but that he sought people "to give themselves to themselves." A self-reliant individual would result. He referred to "the infinitude of the private man." He also preached on the evils of slavery.

The man was strongly influenced by the French essayist Montaigne, and by others who followed the writings of Kant. Those studies led to Emerson's non-traditional ideas of soul and God.

Emerson's body lies in Sleepy Hollow Cemetery, Concord, Massachusetts. Manitoba can be proud that it has honored Emerson: poet, thinker, writer, and leader of the Transcendentalist movement.

However, Emerson had his critics. Algernon Charles Swinburne, critic and poet, described Emerson as "a gap-toothed and hoary-headed ape . . . who now in his dotage spits and chatters from a dirtier perch of his own finding and fouling: coryphaeus or choragus of his Bulgarian tribe of autocopraphagous baboons." Not to be outdone, writer Herman Melville wrote that "I could readily see in Emerson a gaping flaw. It was the insinuation that had he lived in those days when the world was made, he might have offered some valuable suggestions."

Memorable quotes from Ralph Waldo Emerson include:

-And what greater calamity can fall upon a nation than the loss of worship?

-The only reward of virtue is virtue.

-Hitch your wagon to a star.

-If you put a chain around the neck of a slave, the other end fastens itself around your own.

-The greatest man in history was the poorest.

-All men are poets at heart.

-Philanthropies and charities have a certain air of quackery.

-Adopt the pace of nature: her secret is patience.

-Obedience alone gives the right to command.

-The mob is man voluntarily descending to the nature of the beast.

-All mankind love a lover.

-If a man owns land, the land owns him.

-Every hero becomes a bore at last.

-There is properly no history, only biography.

-Fear always springs from ignorance.

-All I have seen teaches me to trust the Creator for all I have not seen.

-Life is not so short but that there is always time enough for courtesy.

-A sufficient measure of civilization is the influence of good women.

The man had his critics. Consider:

-Emerson's writing has a cold, cheerless glitter, like the new furniture in a warehouse, which will come of use by and by.

Alexander Smith, US writer.

-The best answer to his twaddle is *cui bono?* . . . to whom is it a benefit? If not to Mr. Emerson individually, then surely to no man living.

Edgar Allen Poe

At the funeral of fellow-writer Longfellow, Emerson, whose memory was failing, spoke the following: "That gentleman has a sweet, beautiful soul but I have entirely forgotten his name." Emerson blamed his "naughty memory."

Residents of Emerson might tell you of the time writer Ralph Waldo Emerson visited fellow-writer Henry David Thoreau, who was in jail for refusing to pay an 1843 Massachusetts poll tax. Emerson asked his friend: "Henry, why are you here?" Thoreau replied to his visitor: "Waldo, why are you not here?"

---

[1] Transcendentalism suggests that there are modes of being beyond the reach of mundane experience. The term is often associated with Kant, who believed that time, space, and categories of judgment were transcendent: above the evidence of the senses. People like Emerson, Thoreau (the two were friends), and Margaret Fuller, among others, were high-minded and idealistic, putting stress on self-reliance, social reform, and individualism.

Evans Point

By boat or plane, make your way to the north end of Lake Winnipeg and stop at Mossy Point. On the nearby west shore of the Nelson River, you will find Evans Point, named after "a man of the pen and birch bark." Then go a bit north to Norway House to examine the grave of that dynamic individual.

James Evans (1801-1846)

Here was an individual who accomplished much, lived hard, and died young, leaving a mixed and troubling reputation behind him.

James Evans, a Canadian Methodist missionary, educator, writer, and linguist, was born in Kingston-upon-Hull, England to ship's captain James Evans and his wife Mary. At age twenty-one, young James followed his parents to Upper Canada after his schooling in Lincolnshire. He soon converted to Methodism. James accepted a teaching position to the Rice Lake School for Indian children in 1828. Ordained in 1833, he was soon appointed to the St. Clair Mission near Port Sarnia.

On a tour to the north shore of Lake Superior, Evans met the remarkable George Simpson, Governor of the HBC. The Governor appointed Evans to Norway House to preach to and work with natives.

It was in that Manitoba setting that Evans did his finest work. He devised a syllabary for the Ojibwa (1836) and the Cree (1840) languages, which he used in his writing, teaching, and translating. Both syllabaries are based on Pitman shorthand. He often wrote his material on birchbark, which he used as a teaching device. Literacy among natives of the region grew quickly as a result of his efforts. The linguist had a flare for languages.

Over the years, Evans clashed with HBC authorities over its treatment of the native population.

Evans accidentally shot his co-worker and close friend, Thomas Hassall, in 1844. The accident bothered Evans a great deal, and he became increasingly unstable. This man, the missionary who translated parts of the Bible and Christian hymns, was accused of sexual misconduct with native girls under his care.

"The Man Who Made Birchbark Talk" was sent back to London to defend himself. He was acquitted, but the "trial" and stress affected his health. In 1846, James Evans died of a heart attack.

In 1955, the remains of James Evans were brought from England and reburied at Norway House, Manitoba.

Governor General of Canada, Lord Dufferin, said this of Evans: "The nation has given many a man a title, and a pension, and then a resting-place and a monument in Westminster Abbey, who never did half so much for his fellow-creatures."

Image of Rev. James Evans courtesy Provincial Archives, Manitoba Historical Society

Falcon Lake

Drive east from Winnipeg and just before you reach the Manitoba-Ontario border, stop and have an eight-mile swim in Falcon Lake, named in honor of one of Manitoba's earliest song writers: a Canadian original, rhymester,-and Manitopen.

Pierre Falcon (1793-1876)

The Métis song writer and poet was born near today's Swan River to a Cree mother and a French-Canadian father. He was educated in Lower Canada[1] before returning to the prairies, where he married into the famous Cuthbert Grant family. He also served the NWC and the HBC. He was one of the first settlers of Grant's village, now called St. François-Xavier. It is unsure what role he played in the Battle of Seven Oaks. However, he did witness Governor Semple's death during the skirmish.

The songwriter was considered to be the poet or bard of his Métis people. He loved to sing about the bravery of the Bois-brules at Seven Oaks. His music was lively, spirited and full of patriotic sentiment:

> Voulez-vous ecouter chanter
> Une chanson de verite
> Le dix neuf Juin, la bande des Bois-brules
> Sont arrives comme des braves guerriers.

Falcon's music included the ballad *Chanson de la Grenovillére*, which tells us of the political and social issues that affected his people.

Years later (1869-1870), Falcon claimed he was ready to shoulder a gun during the first Riel Resistance or Rebellion.

For nearly fifty years, he lived on the White Horse Plains (see St. Xavier), where he served as justice of the peace.[2]

Alas, most of the music and words sung by Pierre "the Rhymer" Falcon have been lost. What remains is memorable.

> Qui en a fait la chanson?
> Un poete de Canton;
> An bout de la chansoin
> Nous vous le nommeros.
> Un jour etant table
> A boire et a chanter
> A chanter tout an long
> La nouvelle chanson.
> Amis, buvons, trinquons
> Saluons la chanson
> De Pierriche Falcon
> Ce faiseur de chansons.

The last line being often altered to "Pierre Falcon, le bon garçon."

Pierre Falcon and The Census

Appearing at #20 on the 1827 Red River census is:
Pierre Falcon, age 36, Roman Catholic, Rupertsland,
1 married man, 1 woman, 3 sons (-16), 3 daughters (-15),
1 house, 1 stable, 2 cows, 1 calf, 1 swine, 1 cart, 1 canoe,
6 acres, Village of Grant Town or The White Horse Plain.

---

1 Some authorities dispute this point and claim that Falcon could not read and write. A difficult argument.

2 For more details see Don Aiken. *It Happened In Manitoba*. Calgary: Fifth House, 2004, pp 18-23

3 Image of "Pierre the Rhymer" courtesy: Archives of Manitoba

Flin Flon

Can you think of a city, town or village named after a character straight from a science fiction novel? Think Flin Flon! Find the Manitoba settlement nestled by the Saskatchewan border after you drive north from The Pas on Highway #10. Be sure to bring your camera because a certain twenty-four-foot statue awaits your perusal. Call him Flinty.

Flinty

Although Flinty is a product of a writer's imagination, surely you will allow him to be considered an honorary Manitopen.

In 1915, prospector Tom Creighton and friends found a tattered book in the middle of nowhere. Some say the book was half-buried under a rock. The novel by J.E. Preston is called *The Sunless City*, which tells the wild story of one Professor Josiah Flintabbatey Flonatin, a member of the "Society for the Exploration of Unexplored Regions." The 1905 English-published novel tells us that Josiah piloted a submarine through a bottomless lake. Luckily, he found a hole lined with gold. He found the areas's streets lined with gold as well. Coinage was made of tin. Giant Amazon women were in total control. Men were subservient and "kept house."

Creighton, after whom the nearby Saskatchewan settlement was named, discovered rich veins of gold, zinc, copper and silver. He had so enjoyed the damaged Preston book that he called his holdings "Flin Flon" in honor of that literary creation.

Flin Flon – or rather, Flinty – received more publicity when cartoonist Al Capp of *'Lil Abner* fame drew a picture or cartoon of the underwater hero. Later, a statue of Flinty was created, and it now stands proudly in a Flin Flon park.

---

1. Josiah Flintabbatey Flonatin With backpack, flint, and rolling papers in hand, in search of leafy green pastures

Fort Garry

Upper Fort Garry, built in 1822 on the site of Fort Gibraltor (a post of the NWC, 1809-16), was situated at the forks of the Assiniboine and the Red Rivers. Lower Fort Garry was constructed in 1830s, thirty kilometres down the Red River. It was hoped that the second fort would escape the spring flooding sometimes experienced by the old fort.

Both HBC posts were named after Nicholas Garry.

Nicholas Garry (c. 1782-1856)

The English-born son of Isabella Garry and Nicholas Langely took his mother's last name. The boy was raised by his uncle, Thomas Langely, who became a director of the HBC in 1807.

In 1817, Nicholas Garry also became an HBC director. Four years later, the company selected him to visit Canada, where he would supervise the 1821 amalgamation of the HBC and the NWC.

Garry, the administrator, was also a man of the pen: he wrote a diary of his journey and experiences, which later was printed in *The Transactions of the Royal Society of Canada* (1900).

Nicholas Garry served as deputy governor of the HBC from 1822 to 1835. He was relieved of his duties when he "became of unsound mind." The master in chancery managed Garry's affairs until his death at Claygate, Surrey, England.

It is a strange twist, perhaps, that Lower Fort Garry later served as an insane asylum and a penitentiary. Upper Fort Garry was seized by Louis Riel during the 1879 Rebellion-Resistance.

With the decline of the fur trade, the forts named for Nicholas Garry virtually disappeared. Only the gate of the main fort remains today. The restored lower fort is now one of the historic sites of Parks Canada.

It was at Fort Garry and at the neighboring hamlet of Winnipeg that Samuel Steele of NWMP fame had his first view of the old North West. Steele later recalled Winnipeg's only street, which was a trail through the black mud:

> Voyageurs, whites, half breeds and Indians fought, wallowed and slept in all stages of drunkenness, induced by the poison dispenses over the bars of the vile saloons of the place. They made the night and day hideous with their yells, shrieks and curses.[1]

It shall be noted that in 1874 there were only two buildings occupied by white men between Fort Edmonton and Fort Garry: Carlton and Ellice.

Nicholas Garry's diary includes the following entry, which describes an ugly incident at York Factory involving a group of Swiss colonists and some voyageurs, formerly of the NWC.

> Friday, the 24th August. A melancholy occurrence happened today. The Voyageurs or Canadians entered some of the Colonists' Tents and one, a Frenchman, became so intoxicated that he died the next morning. On going to the Encampment I found everything in an Uproar, the Colonists complaining that they had been deceived, that the Canadians had told them that they would be starved to death and a long History of Miseries which had disheartened them.
>
> One Man particularly a Frenchman was at their Head and was very insolent. Suspicions are always wrong but I could not but be surprised to find the two Men of Mr. McGillivray's Canoe, Forcier and Budry (whom he had particularly favored and courted – putting the first at the Head of his Men) in the Camp, and it was evident they were still poisoning the Minds of the People.
>
> I ordered them off the Encampment. They said I was not their Bourgeois. Governor Williams then ordered them. They still refused to go. I then told

Mr. Williams that out of Delicacy to Mr. McGillivray we had better speak to him which we did. But instead of at once ordering them off he reasoned with them and even took their Part.

The Whole Matter was too evident to admit of a Doubt and these men would not have dared to be so impertinent had they not felt they would be supported. The Frenchman was so dangerous a Fellow that I felt if he went to the Colony he would do a great Deal of Mischief. I therefore recommended he should be sent back and his Passage is arranged in the Lord Wellington.

It seems obvious that Garry took his work seriously.

Upper Fort Garry with Red River Expeditionary Force at drill, 1870.
Source: Archives of Manitoba

---

1 Quoted in Pierre Berton *The Wild Frontier*. Toronto: McClelland and Stewart, 1980, p. 86.

Franklin

From Highway #16 between Minnedosa and Neepawa you will spot the settlement of Franklin, named in honor of an individual whose exploits continue to garner both approval and intrigue.

Sir John Franklin (1786-1847)

Here is a man whose diaries, discovered ten years after his death, proved the existence of the Northwest Passage.

John Franklin, born in Spilsby, England, joined the British navy at age fourteen. He fought at the battles of Copenhagen (1801) and Trafalgar (1805).

From 1818, he made extensive journeys along Canada's Arctic coast. He made maps of over 3000 miles of that coast line. On Franklin's second journey (1819-1822), his party ran out of food, so the men were forced to eat the leather parts of their clothing. He returned to England, where he became a national hero. His notes on northern Canada's geology, weather, and plants were well received.

From 1834 to 1845, he was Governor of Van Diemen's Land (Tasmania).

In 1845, at age fifty-nine, Franklin commanded the *Grebus* and the *Terror* in an attempt to discover the Northwest Passage. His crew of 129 officers and men of the Royal Navy carried food, rum, clothing, and tobacco with them – enough to last three years – plus over 2000 books. The 8000 tins of food were sealed with lead, which got into the food. The men suffered a great deal as a result.

Franklin and his men were stopped by thick ice in the Victoria Strait in 1846. He died the next year. Under Captain Crozier, the 105 survivors, using two boats as sledges, attempted to walk to Bock's River, but all died of scurvy and starvation. Canada's north defeated the Franklin endeavor.

In 1847, the first of thirty rescue attempts was made.[1] For thirteen years, Franklin's wife Lady Jane (a plucky, well traveled lady who fought for the rights of female prisoners) spent a fortune financing search parties. Those individuals learned much about survival in Canada's north. They learned from the Inuit, they hunted for food rather than relying on meat from home, and used sledges to advantages.

Between 1850 and 1855, Captain Robert McClure led another search party. He became first to cross the Northwest Passage: by foot, and by ship. Later, Norwegian Roald Amundsen became the first to make the crossing by boat.

It was the diary of John Franklin that first proved the existence of the Northwest Passage.

Today, other nations are claiming that this passage is really "international waters" and must be free to all naval traffic. One wonders what Sir John Franklin might have said about that.

---

[1] One rescue attempt was led by the Nova Scotia-born Edward Belcher. (See Belcher).
Image of John Franklin. Courtesy: Library and Archives Canada C-001352

Gainsborough

Is there room in Manitopens for a gifted artist, a master of light and color? Walk beside or cross Gainsborough Creek, which flows into the Souris River. During your walk, watch for a boy dressed in blue.

Thomas Gainsborough (1727-1788)

If for nothing else, Gainsborough will be remembered for his *Blue Boy*, a haunting study of adolescence. However, that famous painting is only a fraction of the artist's creations.

Gainsborough's father, a prosperous English cloth merchant, realized that the boy had tremendous talent. At age twelve, the lad was sent to London, where he worked with and learned from mature painters. He likely copied and restored Dutch landscapes for dealers. At age nineteen, he married the attractive Margaret Burr who, it appears, brought him a handsome yearly income.

By age twenty-one, Gainsborough was much admired as a landscape painter. His painting *The Charterhouse* showed a mature observation of reality and handling of light. His alternation between invention and observation became the basis of his artistic growth. He had opportunities to study the style and methods of the Dutch master, Anthony Vandyke. Before long, he was ranked with the talented Sir Joshua Reynolds in London. He became famous for the elegance of his portraits, especially of women. Those works have a light and airy quality. Blues and greens dominate his work.

As Gainsborough's excellence increased, so did Reynold's appreciation and approval. The transition of Gainsborough's painting to impressionistic abstraction was described by Reynolds as "chaos assuming form by a kind of magic."

The artist had problems with his portrait of Sarah Siddons. At one sitting, he burst out in exasperation, "Damn your nose, madam, there's no end to it."

Gainsborough painted portraits of such notables as Garrick, Chatterton, Richardson, Foote, Mrs. Siddons, and the Duchess of Devonshire. Some experts rank his *Harvest Wagon* with his *Blue Boy*. He clearly excelled as a landscape painter and portrait painter. Whether the artist painted common folk or the aristocracy, there was a poetically evocative touch to his work.

Gainsborough: a master of light and color. His last words: "We are all going to heaven and Vandyke is of the company." However, his most memorable comment was as follows: "Recollect that painting and punctuality mix like oil and vinegar, and that genius and regularity are utter enemies, and must be to the end of time." The artist also said: "Damn gentlemen. There is not such a set of enemies to a real artist in the world as they are, if not kept at a proper distance."

Residents of southwest Manitoba might tell you of the difficulties experienced by artist Thomas Gainsborough, whom Gainsborough Creek is named after.

Image: Self-portrait painted 1759

GLADSTONE

The town of Gladstone, east of Neepawa, is one of the oldest in Manitoba. The British Prime Minister after whom the town was named was also a serious man-of-the-pen.

WILLIAM EWART GLADSTONE (1809-1898)

The Liverpool-born Liberal statesmen and son of a prosperous tradesman was educated at Eton and Oxford, where he became known as a splendid and witty orator.

In literary history, Gladstone is remembered for his *Studies on Homer and the Homeric Age* (1858), *Juventus Mundi* (1869) and *Homeric Synchronism* (1876). He tried to justify classical studies as the basis of a Christian education.

Gladstone's political writings include *The State in its relations with the Church* (1838), in which he defended the idea of a single state religion. Also to be noted are his *Bulgarian Horrors and the Question of the East* (1876) and *Gleanings of Past Years* (7 vols. 1879), among other articles in periodicals.

Of course, Gladstone the politician is better known than Gladstone the writer.

Memorable quotes from Gladstone include:

-All the world over, I will back the masses against the classes.

-Your business is not to govern the country but it is . . . to call account those who do govern it.
    Speech to the House of Commons, January 29, 1855.

-Swimming for his life, a man does not see much of the country through which the river winds.
    Gladstone's diary, December 31, 1868.

-The proper function of a government is to make it easy for the people to do good and difficult for them to do evil.

-Justice delayed is justice denied.

-Man himself is the crowning wonder of creation.

-Man is to be trained chiefly by studying and by knowing man.

-No man ever became great or good except through many and great mistakes.

-How little do politics affect the life, the moral life of a nation. One single good book influences the people a vast deal more.

-The three highest titles that can be given a man are those of a martyr, hero, saint.

-I do not enter any interior matters. It is so easy to write, but to write honestly is nearly impossible.

-Commerce is the equalizer of the wealth of nations.

-You cannot fight against the future. Time is on our side.
    Speech to the House of Commons, re: the Reform Bill, April 27, 1866.

-The first essential for a Prime Minister is to be a good butcher. (Attributed to Gladstone.)

-My mission is to pacify Ireland.

-Finance is . . . the stomach of the country, from which all the other organs take their tone.

-I absorb the vapor and return it as a flood.
                        Gladstone on public speaking.

-We are part of the community of Europe, and we must do our duty as such.
            House of Commons debates, April 10, 1888.

Comments about Gladstone:

-A sophisticated rhetorician, inebriated with the exuberance of his own verbosity.
>	Benjamin Disraeli on Gladstone.

-He [Labouchere] did not object . . . to Gladstone's always having the ace of trumps up his sleeve, but only to his pretense that God had put it there.

-Gladstone: Mr. Disraeli, you will probably die by the hangman's noose or a vile disease.
 Disraeli: Sir, that depends on whether I embrace your principles or your mistress.

-Gladstone appears to me one of the contemptiblest men I ever looked on . . . almost [a] spectral kind of phantasm of a man . . .
>	Thomas Carlyle, Scottish essayist and historian.

-An old man in a hurry.
>	Lord Randolph Churchill on Gladstone, 1886.

-If Gladstone fell into the Thames, that would be a misfortune, and if anybody pulled him out that, I suppose, would be a calamity.
>	Benjamin Disraeli.

-He speaks to me as if I were a public meeting.
>	Queen Victoria on Gladstone.

-Oh, William dear, if you weren't such a great man, you would be a terrible bore.
>	Gladstone's wife Catherine.

-Mr. Gladstone read Homer for fun, which I think served him right.
>	Winston Churchill.

Gunn Lake

Fly east from Thompson and land your ski plane on the frozen Gunn Lake. The winter weather will determine your departure date. The man after whom the lake was named was a keen observer and recorder of earlier Manitoba weather, and many other facets of the province's history.

Donald Gunn (1797-1878)

Respected historian L.G. Thomas called the historian, educator, scientist, and politician, Donald Gunn, "a genial and humorous man" whose strong opinions and acerbity often criticized the policies of the HBC. Gunn's sympathies clearly focused on the settlers of Manitoba.

The Scot-born Gunn entered the service of the HBC in 1813, and spent ten years at York Factory, Severn Fort and Oxford House. After the NWC and the HBC joined in 1821, he left the company two years later. He then settled at Red River in "Little Britain," later the St. Andrews parish. Earlier, he had married Margaret Swain, a daughter of an HBC officer.

The Gunn family grew to include seven sons and two daughters, who lived in their substantial stone house which doubled as the library serving the Red River region. For eighteen years, Gunn was in charge of the Church Missionary Society's parish school.

The critic of the HBC not only took part in such public affairs, but he also became a spark to the intellectual and cultural life of Red River. The Presbyterian layman was also interested in natural history. He experimented with new strains of wheat and new methods of tillage. His lengthy correspondence with the Smithsonian Institution included his accounts of weather patterns and their effects. For that institution, Gunn made a special exploration west of Lake Winnipeg in 1866, where he collected birds' eggs and skins previously unknown in museums.

That eyewitness to Manitoban history used narrative of events in his writing. He was aware of the danger of "depending for our knowledge of past events on the special pleading of others." His *History of Manitoba* was published posthumously.

Although Gunn often criticized the Roman Catholic and Anglican clergy, he was not considered to be illiberal in outlook. He realized that his duty included a critical evolution of his sources, including his own research.

Gunn also served as a justice of the peace, a police magistrate, inspector of fisheries, postmaster, librarian, and civic leader. He was appointed to the Legislative Council of Manitoba until its 1876 abolition. He was a strong supporter of Canadian federation.

Donald Gunn: a multi-talented Manitopen.

In a November 26, 1885 paper called *The Old Settlers of Red River*, read by George Bryer before the Historical Society, the following comment was included:

> Of those early colonists one name especially occurs to me – that of Donald Gunn, a native of Caithnesshire. He came out with the party of 1813 in the service of the Hudson's Bay Company, and after spending several years on the bay married and settled down in the parish of St. Andrew's. He was a schoolmaster for a time, was a great reader, took much interest in the collections for the Smithsonian Institution – a society to which this society is largely indebted – was a collector of statistics and meteorological data. During his last summer a professor in Boston who was on the astronomical expedition to the Saskatchewan area between 1860 and 70, asked me with much interest of "old Donald Gunn," so familiar a figure in former days in Little Britain. His large family still remain among us.

Obviously, Donald Gunn made his mark on Manitoba.

In Gunn's *History of Manitoba*, there is reference to the great Red River flood of 1852. Gunn's attention to detail is obvious:

> On May 12 . . . about half the colony was inundated and great damage had been done to all property for a distance of over 20 miles up and down the river. The crying of children, the lowing of cattle, squealing of pigs and howling of dogs completed the strange and melancholy scene. Cattle and sheep drowned before people were aware of it and two men who had gone to rest on a rack of hay found themselves in the morning floating with current some three miles from where they had lain down. Others, in the absence of canoes or other assistance had to resort to the housetops, some to the water where they hung to the branches of trees and bushes until daylight brought them relief . . . The cold as well as the water pressed so hard that one man was reduced to the necessity of cutting his plow for firewood to save his children from freezing. Thirty-five hundred souls abandoned their all and took to the open plains. People were huddled together in gypsy groups on every height and hillock that presented itself.[1]

---

1. Quoted in Edith Patterson *Tales of Early Manitoba*. Winnipeg: The Winnipeg Free Press. 1970, p. 20

Image of Donald Gunn. Source: Provincial Archives of Manitoba

Hargrave Lake

Fly east from Flin Flon and land your pontoon plane on Hargrave Lake, named in honor of J.J. Hargrave, the man who wrote *Red River*, a classic of 19th century western Canadian history. The nearby Hargrave River also honors that genuine Manitopen.

Joseph James Hargrave (1841-1894)

The author, journalist, and trader J.J. Hargrave was born in York Factory to HBC Chief Trader James Hargrave and his wife Letitia. Young Joseph was educated in Scotland before returning to Rupert's Land in 1861 as an HBC apprentice clerk and as a secretary to his uncle, William MacTavish, Governor of Assiniboia and of Rupert's Land.

The well connected Hargrave witnessed the Red River uprising-resistance, and expressed his views as a correspondent for the *Montreal Herald*. His weekly articles about the 1869 transfer of Rupert's Land to Canada helped to make his fine reputation.

However, it was Hargrave's book *Red River* that is better remembered and respected. He wrote that the vitality of the fur trade led to the strength of the Red River settlement and its institutions. His 1871 book includes his observations of the social, political, economic, and religious life of the region. He used his father's earlier correspondence with the HBC to great advantage.

Hargrave was later appointed as Chief Trader, a post which allowed him to press for better working conditions for HBC employees. He died shortly after returning to Scotland.

Two items are included here to demonstrate the work of Hargrave, the writer. The first describes Christmas in Red River:

> One of the principal events in the holidays is the celebration of a midnight mass in the cathedral of St. Boniface, on Christmas eve. The large church is brilliantly lighted with several hundreds of candles, the decorations are as gaudy as can be procured, and the music, which is performed by the nuns, and such of the scholars and priests as have any skill in that way, has always been well studied beforehand and is effectively rendered.
>
> The congregation begins to gather from all quarters about an hour before midnight, and the numerous carrioles and cutters, with their bells clearly ringing in the frosty air, create quite an excitement in the dead silence of the winter night. The unusual nature of the solemnity no doubt constitutes the groundwork of its popularity. The advanced hour at which it takes place gives rise to some inconvenience occasionally through the arrival of some noisy worshiper who has been spending a convivial evening with his friends. The doorkeepers, however, usually succeed in dissuading such parties from persevering to effect an entrance.[1]

The second Hargrave item contains an account of the Fort Garry scene as the Winter Packet sets to go:

> The starting of the Northern Packet from Red River is one of the great annual events of the Colony. It occurs generally about 10th December, when the ice having been thoroughly formed and the snow fallen, winter traveling is easy and uninterrupted. The packet arrangements are such that every post in the Northern Department is communicated with through its agency. The means of transit are sledges and snowshoes. The sledges are drawn by magnificent dogs, of which there are

three or four to each vehicle, whose neatly fitting harness, though gaudy in appearance, is simple in design and perfectly adapted to its purposes, while the little bells attached thereto, bright looking and clearly ringing, cheer the flagging spirits of men and animals through the long of a winter day.[2]

Hargrave: a home-grown Manitopen writing about Manitoba!

---

1 J.J. Hargrave. *Red River.* Montreal, John Lovell, 1871, pp 171-73.
2 Ibid.

HARTE

Northeast of Brandon you can visit the settlement called Harte, named after a once-popular writer who, later in his career, found his popularity had decreased: especially in his home country.

(FRANCIS) BRET HARTE (1836-1902)

Harte, born at Albany, New York, was taken to California at age eighteen, where he "mixed" with remaining miners of the gold rush of '49. In San Francisco, he worked on a number of periodicals and newspapers. Some of Harte's earlier stories were printed in those periodicals.

Most well known of Harte's short stories were collected in the *Luck of Roaring Camp* (1868). His humorous-pathetic verse included *Plain Language from Truthful James* (1870) often referred to as "the Heathen Chinee", among others.

Harte was appointed American consul in Germany (1878-80) and at Glasgow (1880-85). He then moved to England, where he continued his writing. Many critics claimed that that work was repetitious and not equal to his earlier endeavors. Certainly in his home country, his appeal had sharply decreased.

Some of the memorable quotes from Harte include:

> -If, of all words of tongue and pen,
> the saddest are, "It might have been,"
> More sad are these we daily see:
> "It is, but hadn't ought to be!"

> -And he smiled a kind of sickly smile, and curled up on the floor,
> And the subsequent proceedings interested him no more.

-All you know about it [luck] for certain is that it's bound to change.

The man was even less popular than his work, according to his contemporary, Mark Twain. Here are four such comments from Twain:

-He was showy, meretricious, insincere; and he constantly advertised these qualities in his dress. He was distinctly pretty, in spite of the fact that his face was badly pitted with smallpox. In the days when he could afford it – and in the days when he couldn't – his clothes always exceeded the fashion by a shade or two.

-He was an incorrigible borrower of money; he borrowed from all his friends; if he ever repaid a loan the incident failed to pass into history.

-He hadn't a sincere fiber in him. I think he was incapable of emotion for I think he had nothing to feel with.

-Harte, in a mild and colorless way, was that kind of man – that is to say, he was a man without a country. No, not man. Man is too strong a term. He was an invertebrate without a country. He hadn't any more passion for his country than an oyster has for its bed; in fact not so much and I apologize to the oyster

---

Portrait of Bret Harte by John Pettie (1884)

Heming Lake

East and a bit south of Flin Flon is a railway point named in honor of the gifted Canadian artist, illustrator, and writer Arthur Heming.

Arthur Heming (1870-1940)

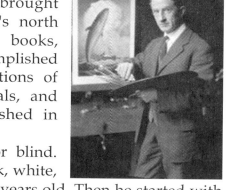

Born in Paris, Ontario, and raised in Hamilton, the "chronicler of the North," Arthur Heming, brought vivid depictions of Canada's north to the world. His essays, books, paintings, and sketches accomplished that task. Heming's illustrations of northern trappers, aboriginals, and wildlife were widely published in North America and Europe.

Arthur Heming was color blind. As a result he painted in black, white, and yellow until he was sixty years old. Then he started with other glorious colors on works that really made his reputation. *Toronto Telegram* critic Kenneth Wells described Heming's art as a real and honest expression of the Canadian north:

> There is more of the north in them, more real Canadianism, as the landscape painters understand it, than in the whole lumped output of the Group of Seven. His pictures may not appeal to the sophisticates of the studio . . . Gallery curators may not find them satisfying to that snobbism which breeds in such places . . . In a modernistic wilderness of self-expression he puts self aside to accurately describe on canvas the life of a northland that is passing and that will soon be only a dream . . . he paints the north not as a painter loving color and design for its own sake, but as an artist loving it for his subject's sake.

The man's pen was also busy. Using his northern experiences, he published three novels: *The Living Forest*, *Spirit Lake* and *The Drama of the Forests*.

Arthur Heming, a multi-talented Canadian whose works should be better known in Canada and beyond! However, he leaves us with this comment from *The Drama of the Forests*:

> Though the female always runs away, she never runs so fast that she couldn't run faster; and it makes no difference whether the female has wings or fins, flippers or feet, it is all the same – the female always does the courting.

Image: Arthur Heming 1912

Herchmer

Herchmer, northwest of York Factory (the oldest permanent settlement in Manitoba), was named in honor of the first civilian to serve as Commissioner of the NWMP: a man with a sharp pen and a quick mind.

Lawrence Herchmer (1840-1915)

Herchmer, once described as a flinty-eyed martinet, served as NWMP Commissioner from 1886 to 1900. Earlier, the English-born Herchmer served as a supply officer for the British Boundary Commission (defining the Canada-USA border) and as Indian Agent in Manitoba.

As the nation's top policeman, he was initially considered to be a capable administrator who organized the police force into an efficient police service. He stressed excellent training, better living conditions, and better benefits for the police force.

However, many members of the force considered Herchmer an "outsider." One veteran wrote that when the preceding Commissioner Leif Crozier was replaced by the non-policeman Herchmer, the action "was regretted by all his companions in the force."[1]

Herchmer often considered the slightest complaint against his orders to be an act of insubordination. His quick temper and overbearing personality created numerous enemies. Later, he was publically charged with tyrannical conduct and mismanagement. A judicial inquiry cleared him of the serious charges. However, while serving the Canadian Rifles during the Boer War, he was replaced as Commissioner. For the rest of his life, Herchmer considered his dismissal to have been an unfair action.

It was Lawrence Herchmer who announced to a public gathering in Regina that the incident involving Almighty Voice (see the section entitled *After the Violence*) was a dangerous one, indeed. Here is one description of Herchmer exercising his authority:

> The commissioner, a stocky figure with a square face and a grizzled beard, walked to the center of the dance floor, held up his hand to stop the music, and spoke: "I have here a telegram stating that Captain Allan, whom you all know, has been shot and seriously wounded and some others have been killed by the Indians near Duck Lake.[2]

The Commissioner sharply concluded his short speech by adding that "the police have other things to do besides dancing. The rigs will be at the door to take you to your horses." Herchmer worked through the night, and by his orders a CPR special train left at 6 a.m. from Regina to Duck Lake. Under his orders, a train carried a nine-pound maxim gun, thirteen horses, twenty-five men, and Assistant Commissioner John McIllree, a man described as a fierce-looking man with a monstrous cavalry mustache.

Herchmer was afraid of another Indian uprising. He sent telegrams to the commanders of police posts at Battleford, Calgary, Edmonton, Macleod, Maple Creek and Lethbridge. The telegrams stated: "In attempting to arrest Mighty Voice, three men are killed and Insp. Allan and four men are wounded and one Indian killed. Explain matters to Indians and get ready in case of further trouble." The Commissioner's subsequent actions should be noted:

> Herchmer ordered the Prince Albert division to ship half a ton of bully beef to the bluff plus a half ton of hard tack from Winnipeg. From Duck Lake he ordered half a ton of oats for the horses, fifty pounds of bread, and forty pounds of fresh beef for the men. He placed an order for an additional one hundred shells for the Maxim gun and ordered

Gagnon at Prince Albert to swear in as many special constables as needed. And he asked permission of the Indian department in Ottawa to swear in fifty Blackfoot and Blood Indian scouts as well, for service in the north. The Blackfoot and Bloods had taken no part in the Rebellion of '85.[3]

One can see that Herchmer was decisive and determined. He died a rather bitter man in Vancouver. He was a leader who insisted that his men act by the book and tradition. He wrote that the Force would always cause its men to risk their lives rather than run the risk of being tried for manslaughter. Herchmer stressed that the Force's tradition was inviolable, and police must not "use unnecessary violence."

If Herchmer over-reacted in the Almighty Voice incident, he was mirroring public opinion as expressed by the *Regina Standard*: "Are We On The Verge of Another Indian Outbreak?" Herchmer took no chances! The 1897 incident best describes the man and his actions.

> Lawrence Herchman possessed a cannon-ball head and a projectile-like nature that exploded all opposition. His reddish beard concealed a steel jaw backed by an imperious will. Behind all lurked an immense comprehension of the west and a passionate admiration for the Mounted Police . . . he was feared, disliked, hated, admired, loved, and obeyed. He knew how to look after his men.[4]

---

1 The writer was Sir Cecil E. Denny. See his *The Law Marches West*.
Note: Herchmer, an angry man, wrote to fellow policeman Sam Steele asking "what authority had you for buying so many potatoes in May [at the Battleford]?"
2 Pierre Berton. *The Wild Frontier*. Toronto: McClelland and Stewart. 1980, pp 238-239.
3 Berton. p. 239
   Note: York Factory is often called "the cradle of the west."
4. T. Morris Longstreth. *The Scarlet Force*. Ottawa: The Canadiana Co.mpany, 1953, p. 152,

Hudson Bay

Manitoba, the Keystone province, has long had connection to the rest of the world thanks to that "sea" we call Hudson Bay. Yes, there are seas smaller than the bay named after "the keeper of the ship's log." Therein lies a story of tragedy.

Henry Hudson (c. 1570-1611)

You might call Hudson the founder of New York City and of the Hudson's Bay Company. But is this overstatement? (Very little is known of his earliest years.)

He searched for a polar route to Asia via Norway and Russia twice without success (1607, 1608). In the service of the Dutch East India Company, he ascended the Hudson River in 1609 as far as today's Albany, New York state.

English patrons financed his search for the Northwest Passage in 1610. His ship, the *Discovery*, left for Iceland and then went on to the Hudson Strait in June. He descended the eastern shore into James Bay in his desperate attempt to reach the Spice Islands and the Far East. He believed he was then in the Pacific Ocean. It was a tough, bleak winter when he beached his boat.

Displeased with their "living conditions" and Hudson's leadership and decisions, a number of the crew mutinied. Hudson, his twelve-year old son, and seven others were forced into a shallop, which was cut adrift in the open on June 23, 1611. Those nine people were never again seen.

Hudson didn't discover the Hudson Strait, but he did find a route to the continent's interior. The "opening" of the Hudson Bay was of inestimable value for England. His written log and charts are of interest to many historians.

Navigator Robert Bylot, a member of Hudson's crew, led the Discovery safely back to England (they were driven to eat bird's bones fried in candle grease). For that reason, Bylot (who had further trips to the Arctic with Button and Baffin) was not charged with mutiny. Four others were arraigned, but were eventually acquitted.

A brilliant observation can be noted here: "Hudson was a man in whom courage, vision, and intensity of purpose were vitiated by lack of the more commonplace qualities of good leadership . . . his trouble was chiefly with his officers."[1]

Other relevant quotes:

-I would rather be hanged at home than starved abroad.
> Henry Greene, one of the leaders of the mutiny.

-The disastrous voyage of Henry Hudson had one substantial result: a new company was formed. "the Discovers of the North-west Passage." In its list of 288 [mostly rich] members [were] the names of Bylot, Prickett and Wilson": members of Hudson's crew.
> George Malcolm Thomson, p. 83.

-He [Hudson] was a failure for two reasons, once because he could not dominate his unruly crew and again because he did not find the northern seaway to Asia.
> George Malcolm Thomson, p. 84.

-Single-handed Hudson blazed the way through the 400 miles of his strait and opened up the vast tract on inland sea beyond.[3]
> Neatby, p. 378

Almost as large as the Mediterranean Sea, Hudson Bay has a shoreline of approximately 7,600 miles: a distance not much shorter than the earth's diameter at the equator. It was through that north-central "side door" that the earliest British "occupation" of Canada took place.

---

1 L.H. Neatby. "Henry Hudson." *Dictionary of Canadian Biography*, Vol. I. p. 378.
Note: Digges, south of Fort Churchill, was named after Sir Dudley Digges, who helped to finance Hudson's explorations. Digges Island also honors his name.

HUGO

Southeast of Neepawa, you should stop at a railway point named after the towering talent called Victor Hugo. Bring a comfortable chair, and under a warm Manitoba sun, reread some of your favorite stories by Hugo: novelist, poet, and dramatist.

VICTOR HUGO (1802-1885)

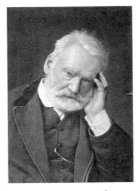

In print and on stage and screen, Victor Hugo's *Les Misérables* has entertained and enlightened millions of people worldwide. The author's intent was to show the threefold problem of his century: the destruction of children, the degradation of proletarian man, and the fall of woman through hunger and hopelessness. His characters, Jean Valjean and the waif Gavroche, among others, won Hugo a vast readership. The 1862 publication was a love story and a mystery. Social injustice was the core of the story.

Who was this man, Hugo, whose pen produced poems, plays, novels, satires, dramas, epics, and on and on; not to exclude the novel, *Notre Dame de Paris* (1830)? There, we read of Quasimodo the hunchback, Esmeralda the gypsy girl, Frollo the archdeacon, and others. Yes, who was this man with a vision of mystical grandeur, remarkable versatility, and the breadth of creation?

The erratically schooled Hugo experienced a nomadic early life. He began his serious writing while an adolescent, because he wanted to "escape the ordinary life." In 1882, he married his childhood sweetheart, Adele Foucher, with whom he had four children. He celebrated his love for Adele in posting his first signed book, in which he wrote: "Poetry is the most intimate of all things." Hugo, the romanticist, used Shakespeare, the Bible, and Homer as his chief sources.

He and other young writers found richness and beauty in the Medieval Period.

Often, his immense egoism ("Ego Hugo" was his motto) and his deep melancholy bothered his family and friends. Tormented by what he considered his wife's coldness – and by his inordinate sexual cravings – Hugo fell in love with a young actress, Juliette Drouet, who lived in his shadow for fifty years. When he was eighty, one of his grandsons surprised him in the arms of a young laundress. A very cool Hugo announced: "Look Little George, this is what they call genius."

Hugo's changing political beliefs brought him to the English Channel Islands, Guernsey (where he often swam naked, and where he installed his mistress not far from the home he and his wife shared) and Jersey, where he experienced the supernatural. Under the influence of a female voyante, he believed he communicated with the spirits of Shakespeare, Racine, Dante, and even Jesus. The séance that affected him most was the "visit" he had with his daughter, who had drowned years earlier. Juliette stayed loyal to him during the seventeen years he was away from the mainland. His wife had left him earlier. Hugo's mysticism and belief in reincarnation affected his life and his relationships.

Initially, Hugo supported Napoleon III, who was later removed after France's defeat in the Franco-Prussian War. Hugo wrote: "Because we have had a Great Napoleon, we must now have a Little One?" So Hugo returned to Paris.

If Hugo found life to be a struggle, an unfair struggle, then that sentiment is surely found in the character Jean Valjean, one of literature's great creations.

How many people have known injustices such as were experienced by the "convict" Jean Valjean? Hugo had many observation worth reading:

-I am for religion against religions.

-The sewer is the conscience of the city.

-Who stops revolution half way? The bourgeoisie.

-God made himself man: granted. The Devil made himself woman.

-An invasion of armies can be resisted; an invasion of ideas cannot be resisted.

-A fixed idea ends in madness or heroism.

-Envy is an admission of inferiority.

-And now, Lord God, let us explain ourselves to each other.

-We are all under the sentence of death, but with a sort of indefinite reprieve.

-If we must suffer, let us suffer nobly.

-Adversity makes men, and prosperity makes nonsense.

-God made only water, but man made wine.

-Symmetry is tedious, and tedium is the very basis of mourning. Despair yawns.

-The word is the Verb and the Verb is God.

-Kings are for nations in their swaddling clothes.

Southwest of Gimli is the settlement called Inwood. Its earlier name was Cosette. Some people believe that name originated with Hugo's little girl, Cosette, in *Les Misérables*.

Hugo residents might tell you that writer Victor Hugo wanted to know what his publishers thought of his manuscript of *Les Misérables*. He sent them a note simply reading: "?" They replied: "!"

INGELOW

Early in the 20th century, the Woodlea district, northeast of Brandon, became the Ingelow district. Railroad officials chose to honor the English poetess and novelist, Jean Ingelow, in such a fashion.

JEAN INGELOW (1820-1897)

When Lord Alfred Tennyson read Ingelow's first volume, *A Rhyming Chronicle of Incidents and Feelings*, he called the work "charming." They later became friends.

The precocious Lincolnshire-born daughter of a banker contributed tales and verses to magazines earlier, but it was her 1863 *Poems* that made her a popular writer. Some of the items were set to music to be sung in drawing rooms in America, as well as her England.

In the late 1860s and later, Jean Ingelow became a productive and popular novelist. Some of her work was directed at children, who found it delightful.

Some critics, however, found her song-poems to be stilted and affected. She "overwrote," some claimed. Nevertheless, Ingelow had a gift for the narrative, and a good way of creating characters. She was not an affected person, and was seen by others as a hospitable, frank individual.

Tennyson continued to praise the poetess-novelist. After reading more of her work, the great man – in that now legendary phrase – said to her: "Miss Ingelow, I do declare you do the trick better than I do."

When Tennyson died, many people believed that Jean Ingelow should have been chosen Poet Laureate in his place. However, Queen Victoria was likely averse to having a female poet in that post.

The poetess had other disappointments, of course. She had an unrequited love affair with a sailor who had promised marriage. He never returned from his next trip abroad.

The earlier mentioned "Feelings" poem was likely influenced by that turn of events.

Many critics claim that her most celebrated poem, *High Tide on the Coast of Lincolnshire* (1571), is her best effort. Ingelow's poetry and stories continue to be enjoyed.

Here are quotes from Ingelow:

-Youth, youth, how buoyant are thy hopes; they turn
Like marigolds, toward the sunny side.
       From: *The Four Bridges*.

Crowds of bees are giddy with clover
Crowds of grasshoppers skip at our feet,
Crowds of larks at their matins hang over,
Thanking the Lord for a life so sweet.
         From: *Divided*

But two are walking apart forever
And wave their hands for a mute farewell.
        From: *Divided*.

A sweeter woman ne'er drew breath
Than my sonne's wife, Elizabeth.
  From: *The High Tide on the Coast of Lincolnshire*.

Man dwells apart, though not alone,
He walks among his peers unread;
The best of thoughts which he hath known
For lack of listeners are not said.
        From: *Afterthought*

How short our happy days appear!
How long the sorrowful!
      From: *The Mariner's Cave*.

To bear, to nurse, to rear
To watch and then to lose,
To see my bright ones disappear,
Drawn up like morning dews.
     From: *Songs of Seven. Seven times Six*.

JUSTICE

You will find Justice a bit to the northeast of Brandon. The settlement's earlier name was Aikenside, which took that name from a country school called Aikenside. A local teacher there had chosen that name for her school, because she had recently read a book by that name written by teacher-turned-author, Mary Jane Holmes.

MARY JANE HOLMES (1825-1907)

This individual taught school at the age of thirteen. The Brookfield, Massachusetts-born Mary Jane Hawes married Daniel Holmes, a lawyer, who took his family to Versailles, Kentucky.

Holmes' first novel, *Tempest and Sunshine*, pictured southern society. *English Orphans* followed in the next year. Her earlier work received only moderate favor. However, many books followed as her reputation grew. By 1887, Holmes had written twenty-eight novels (some people referred to such work as "dime novels") and numerous articles. Some of her books attained a sale of 50 000 copies.

Holmes' stories about domestic life were "pure in tone and free from sensational incidents" without having an avowedly moral purpose. With the exception of Harriet Beecher Stowe, no female American author had received such large profits from her copyright. Before appearing in book form, some of her work was published as serials in the *New York Weekly*. By then, she had made Brockport, New York, her home.

Her *Lena Rivers* became a tremendous best seller, making her one of the most popular writers of her day.

According to her critics, Holmes' stories were love stories pure and simple, and were based upon overwrought emotional situations. The same critics thought her to be far too incompetent a writer to cast aside the customary aids of forged letters, accidental meetings, and disguises. Her strength consisted in creating the most artificial tragedies that her heroines would suffer. The term "sensational fiction" came to mind, according to critics.

A list of Holmes' books includes:

Tempest and Sunshine (New York, 1854)
The English Orphans (1855)
The Homestead on the Hillside, and other Tales (Auburn, 1855)
Lena Rivers (1856)
Meadow Brook (New York, 1857)
Dora Dean or the East India Uncle (1858)
Maggie Miller, or Hagar's Secret (1858)
Cousin Maude and *Rosamond* (1860)
Marian Grey (1863)
Hugh Worthington (1863)
Darkness and Daylight (1864)
The Cameron Pride, or Purified by Suffering (1867)
The Christmas Font, a story for young folks (1868)
Rose Mather, a Tale of the War (1868)
Ethelyn's Mistake (1869)
Millbank (1871)
Edna Browning (1872)
West Lawn, and the Rector of St. Mark's (1874)
Mildred (1877)
Daisy Thornton (1878)
Forest House (1879)
Chateau d'or (1880)
Red Bird (1880)
Madeline (1881)"
Queenie Hatherton (1883)
Christmas Stories (1884)
Bessie's Fortune (1885)
Gretchen (1887)

Perhaps the following quote from Holmes' *Aikenside* will do justice to the residents of Justice:

> The good people of Devonshire were rather given to quarreling – sometimes about the minister's wife, meek, gentle Mrs. Tiverton, whose manner of housekeeping, and style of dress, did not exactly suit them; sometimes about the minister himself, good patient Mr. Tiverton, who vainly imagined that if he preached three sermons a week, attended the Wednesday evening prayer-meeting, the Thursday evening sewing society, officiated at every funeral, visited all the sick, and gave to every beggar who called at his door, besides superintending the Sunday school, he was earning his salary of six hundred per year.
>
> Sometimes, and that not rarely, the quarrel crept into the choir, and then, for one whole Sunday, it was all in vain that Tiverton read the psalm and hymn, casting troubled glances toward the vacant seats of his refractory singers. There was no one to respond, unless it were good old Mr. Hodges, who pitched so high that few could follow him; while Mrs. Captain Simpson – whose daughter, the organist, had been snubbed at the last choir meeting by Mr. Hodges' daughter, the alto singer – rolled up her eyes at her next neighbor, or fanned herself furiously in token of her disgust.

How would that prolific author sell today?

---

1 "Appleton's Encyclopedia"
Image Source: University of Virginia Library, Electronic Text Center

Kelsey

The long rail line from The Pas to Churchill sends a spur line north to the Kelsey community, east of Split Lake. Henry Kelsey, after whom the area was named, surely deserves a prominent city, place, river, lake or district to be named after him, as well.

Henry Kelsey (c. 1667-1724)

Explorer Henry Kelsey, a giant in western Canadian history, came to York Factory at age fourteen to work for the HBC. A number of "firsts" are attributed to the English-born explorer-map maker-journal writer: the first European to see the Canadian prairies and their buffalo (bison), and the first to describe the grizzly bear. He was to serve the HBC for nearly forty years: all but three of them at Hudson Bay.

The governor of the HBC was directed to "send the boy Henry Kelsey to Churchill River because we are informed he is a very active lad delighting much in Indian company, being never better pleased than when he is traveling amongst them."[1] Later, Kelsey and a young Cree Indian were set ashore on the west coast of Hudson Bay. From there, they began their overland journey to search for the Buffalo River and to attract the northern Indians to the fur-trading posts. They penetrated about 150 miles inland before returning to York Factory.

Kelsey is best remembered for his 1690-92 trip to the west to "call, encourage, and invite remoter Indians to trade with us."[2] He travelled through Cedar Lake, and up the Saskatchewan River, then on to a site near today's The Pas. From there, Kelsey's party of Assiniboine Indians journeyed southwest to the prairies of today's Saskatchewan, where he found "nothing but beast and grass." It was a land fabulously rich in beaver pelts. While there, he heard stories from local natives of "a great wall of mountains" (the Rockies) to the west.

During his two-year stay on the prairies, Kelsey compiled a Cree dictionary so that traders could learn that language.

The explorer's reward for loyal service was his appointment as chief trader at Albany (1705) and governor of all the Bay posts (1718-22). He was the first known trader to be allowed to take an Indian wife into an HBC fort.

The HBC then failed to follow up Kelsey's discoveries by not establishing inland posts for trading purposes. The company expected the Indians to make long trading trips to the Hudson Bay area (the French did a better job in that regard).

During his travels, Kelsey kept a journal that is sometimes difficult to read and understand. He wrote part of his journals in rhyme:

> In sixteen hundred and ninety't years
> I set forth as plainly may appear.
>
> At Deering's Point after the frost
> I set up there a certain cross.[3]

Another quote from Kelsey's journal:

> -Abundance of Musketers [mosquitoes] and at night could not gett wood Enough for to make a smoke to clear ym.

It is interesting to note that the 1684 sailing vessel named *Happy Return* which left England for York Factory had two passengers who became famous for their endeavors in western Canada. One was the experienced Pierre Radisson (1636-1710) and the other, the fourteen-year-old apprentice named Henry Kelsey, who richly deserves the compliment "Manitopen."

Note: Although not a noted man of the pen, the French-born Médard Chovart Des Groseilliers (after whom the railway point northwest of Wabowden was named) should be mentioned here because he is so much a part of the diary-journal of his much younger brother-in-law, Pierre-Esprit Radisson. They are usually mentioned in tandem; the two "Caesars of the Wilderness" were the first to explore Lake Superior in detail, first to negotiate treaties with the Crees (Kiristinon in French), and first to explore the upper reaches of the Missouri and Mississippi Rivers. Their discoveries and plans for transportation routes for the fur trade led to the founding of the Hudson's Bay Company. Radisson (1636-1710) and Des Groseilliers (1618-1696?) served both the French and the English. The two fur traders switched alliances according to the treatment they received from the two nations. Des Groseilliers valued courage, freedom, and initiative. He and Radisson donned "native dress" when they met King Charles II in England, where countless citizens were dying from the bubonic plague. The enterprising pair showed Prince Rupert and other investors the value of the Hudson Bay route to the fur trade. It was Radisson, whose diary-journal told of the pair's exploits, who boasted: "We were Caesars, being nobody to contradict us." Most experts today consider the two fortune hunters to have been Canada's greatest coureurs de bois. School children still refer to them as Radishes and Gooseberries.

Incidentally, Gillam, Manitoba, is named for Zachariah Gillam, Captain of the *Nonsuch*.

---

1 Quoted D.C. Willows and S. Richmond. *Canada: Colony to Centennial.* Toronto: McGraw Hill, 1970, p. 77
2 Ibid.
3 No one today knows where Deering Point was situated. The Kelsey papers dated 1693 were not "discovered" until 1926.

Knox

Knox is a railway point north of Brandon, named in honor of a man with a single-minded zeal but also with a mind often closed to tolerance.

JOHN KNOX (C. 1505-1572)

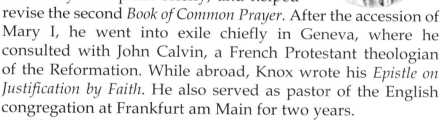

The outstanding leader of the Scottish Reformation, John Knox, likely attended the University of St. Andrews before becoming a Catholic priest. He came in contact with George Wishart, a strong supporter of the Lutheran Reformation. Knox then became a Protestant.

Knox preached in England (1549-54), was a royal chaplain briefly, and helped revise the second *Book of Common Prayer*. After the accession of Mary I, he went into exile chiefly in Geneva, where he consulted with John Calvin, a French Protestant theologian of the Reformation. While abroad, Knox wrote his *Epistle on Justification by Faith*. He also served as pastor of the English congregation at Frankfurt am Main for two years.

John Knox returned to Scotland in 1559, now known for his *First Blast of the Trumpet Against the Monstrous Regiment of Women*.[1] As a minister in Edinburgh, he tried to abolish the authority of the Pope while condemning the creeds and practices of the old church. He attacked the religion of Mary, Queen of Scots, and her fellow Catholics. Her abdication led to the establishment of the Church of Scotland.

The founder of Scottish Presbyterianism was part-author of the *First Book of Discipline*, in which he advocated a national system of education ranging from a school in every parish to the three universities. His *Treatise on Predestination* was published in 1560. For a long time, he wrote his *History of the Reformation of Religion within the Realm of Scotland*, a book published after his death.

John Knox had two sons by his wife Marjory Bowes, who died in 1560. Four years later, he married the very young Margaret Stewart, with whom he had three daughters.

The reformer was not a man to be easily dismissed. His individualism, determination, wit, native humor, and shrewd worldly sense served him well. He was either hostile or indifferent to people and ideas of a different nature. His attitude towards women anger people today. Memorable quotes from Knox include:

-To promote a Woman to beare rule, superiorities, dominion, or empire above any Realme, nation, or Citie, is repugnant to Nature; contumelie to God, a thing most contrarious to his reveled will and approved ordinance; and finallie, it is the subversion of good Order, of all equitie and justice . . . For who can denie but it is repugnant to nature, that the blind shall be appointed to leade and conduct such as do see? That the weake, the sicke, and impotent persons shall norishe and kepe the hole and strong? And finalie, that the foolishe, madde, and phrenetike shall governe the discrete, and give counsel to such as be of sober mind? Of such be all women, compared unto man in bearing of authorie. For their sight in civile regiment is but blindnes; their strength, weaknes, their counsel, foolishnes; and judgement, phrensie, if it be rightlie considered . . .

-Queen Mary: Think ye that subjects, having the power, may resist their princes?
Knox: If their princes exceed their bounds, Madam, no doubt they may be resisted, even by power.

-Un homme avec Dieu est toujours dan la majorité.
(A man with God is always in the majority.)

-The nobility both of England and Scotland are inferior to brute beasts, for they do that to women which no male among the common sort of beasts can be proved to do the their females: that is, they reverence them, and quake at their presence; they obey their commandments, and that is against God.

-Nature, I say, doth paynt them [women] further to be weak, fraile, impacient, feble, and foolish; and experience hath declared them to be unconstant, variable, cruell, and lacking the spirit of council and regiment.

-Cursed Jezebel of England.

Knox on Queen Mary I.

-Dorothy Parker wrote:

Whose love is given over-well
Shall look on Helen's face in hell,
Whilst they whose love is thin and wise
May view John Knox in paradise,

---

1 Regiment here has its old sense of "rule, magisterial authority" and has no connection with the military.

Kulish

Drive a few minutes north from Grandview, and be greeted by residents of the community called Kulish, named in honor of the introverted Ukrainian intellectual and writer, Panteleimon Kulish, a romantic of the first order.

Panteleimon Kulish (1819-1897)

Kulish, poet, translator, writer, historian and ethnographer, was born into an impoverished Cossack-gentry family. The fine student was not allowed to finish his university studies because he was not a noble. In his twenties, he wrote his first historical novel in Russian: *Little Russia Eighty Years Ago* (2 vols.). He also published his epic poem, *Ukrainia*. He taught school for a time while studying Ukrainian ethnography and history.

In 1845 Kulish accepted a position at Saint Petersburg University, where he wrote his major historical novel, *The Black Council*. Other novels, biographies, and poems followed.

Ukrainian interests held sway in his mind. Kulish began the translation of the Bible, the works of Byron, Goethe, and Shakespeare.

Kulish was thought by some people to be an egocentric man with uncompromising attitudes. He stressed the development of a separate, indigenous Ukrainian culture, while advocating political union with Russia. Ukrainian populists strongly disagreed. However, the controversial Kulish produced an astonishing list of writing and publishing activities. Those activities were not aided by his arrest by Tsarist police for allegedly belonging to the Cyril and Metodius Brotherhood. After two months in prison, he was exiled for three years to Tula. His loss of freedom, closed trial, and stiff interrogation were deeply traumatic for him. His wife, the writer Hanna Barvinok, supported him all the way.

Kulish, often called "Ukraine's truly European intellectual," moved and worked in literary circles which included Taras Shevchenko[1], Vasyl Bilozersky, and Mykola Kostromariev, among others.

While his critics have disagreed with Kulish on political and social concerns, few would fail to grant him his achievements.

---

[1] Vita, a settlement near Steinbach, was earlier called Szewczenko in his honor.

Landseer

Between Glenboro and Cypress River on Highway #2 lies the community of Landseer, named in honor of a brilliant painter who had a lifetime of bad health and depression.

Edwin Henry Landseer (1802-1873)

Edwin was one of the fourteen children of John Landseer, who taught all his children the skill of engraving. At age four, Edwin began sketching, and by age fourteen he was admitted to the Royal Academy Schools in London. Ten years later, he was elected an Associate of the Academy at the earliest age possible for an artist to receive that honor. He became a full Academician when not yet thirty years old.

Landseer, a brilliant animal painter, seemed to give his animal scenes a moral dimension. His pictures were widely circulated in the form of engravings, some made by his brother Thomas.

In 1824, the young painter made his first visit to Scotland. He fell in love with the countryside. Many other visits followed. The country's history impressed him more and more as time went on. The Highlands were prominent in his paintings. He also painted portraits of well-known Scots. Sir Walter Scott's portrait was one of Landseer's most famous works.

Landseer loved animals, especially sheepdogs of Scotland. His animal pictures became very popular in Victorian England. When the Queen and Prince Albert also "discovered" Scotland, Landseer enjoyed royal patronage. In 1850, he began a large group portrait of the royal family. Unfortunately, the work was never finished. The Queen knighted him in spite of that fact.

That "failure" partly caused his breakdown in 1840. In spite of poor mental and physical health, he continued his work for many more years. The aristocracy and richer business people scrambled to buy the man's works.

In the 1860s, he modeled the lions at the base of Nelson's Column in Trafalgar Square, London.

For the last two years or so of his life, Edwin Landseer sank slowly into madness.

Let Sir Walter Scott[1] have the last word: "Landseer's dogs were the most magnificent things I ever saw."

---

[1] Scott chose Landseer as one of the illustrators to the Waverley edition of his novels. (See Scott).

Munk

The Munk River flows northeast into the Churchill River. The Munk settlement, situated a bit southeast of Gillam, is named after the same individual.

Jens Eriksen Munk (Munck) (1579-1628)

Here is another intrepid explorer who wielded a busy pen. The Danish sailor made landfall at a spot later called Cape Churchill, Manitoba, where he found shelter for his ships. the weather forced him to spend the winter of 1619-20 at the estuary of the Churchill River. He called that estuary *Jens Muncke's Bay*. During that long winter, Munk's busy pen recorded a number of scientific observations and opinions regarding the origins of the icebergs, an eclipse of the moon, bird migration, parhelions, and other astronomical occurrences.

Munk was born near Barbo, Norway. His early years were spent at sea, and later, during the 1611-13 war with Sweden, he was commissioned a captain in the Danish navy. He then fulfilled various duties at the request of his sovereign, Christian IV. He became interested in whaling, and he introduced the industry to Denmark.

Christian IV was very interested in the Northwest Passage, so he instructed Munk to make a voyage in search of it. Munk took two ships, the *Lamprey* and the *Narwhal,* or *Unicorn*[1], and sailed north of the Shetlands, past the Faroes, past the coast of Greenland, and then west to northern Canada. By July 8, 1619, he had sighted the western shore of Davis Strait. He sailed into Frobisher Bay thinking it was Hudson Strait. Then Munk sailed south to Hudson Strait, but he named it *Fretum Christian*.

Munk and his sixty-one crew members (including his twelve-year-old son) anchored and went ashore to meet with the natives and to hunt bear, reindeer, and birds. He took possession of the land in the name of Christian IV, setting up the king's arms and monogram.

In August, Munk sailed to Ungava Bay, wrongly thinking it was Hudson Bay. He later entered Hudson Bay. He called the whole area *Novum Mare Christian*. Then he sailed south where, as mentioned earlier, he wrote his scientific observations while foraging in the countryside. By January 1620, Munk's men were beginning to succumb to scurvy. His ships had adequate supplies of medicines, herbs, and waters, but no one knew how to administer them. By June, only Munk and two crew members remained alive. In their weakened condition, the three men sailed the *Lamprey* back to Copenhagen, 3500 miles away: an amazing epic of endurance. Like so many others, Munk failed to find the Northwest Passage.

At home, he published his account of his voyage to the Hudson Bay region. He made plans to return to the area with colonists and to establish a fur trade. For many reasons, including financial, nothing resulted from these plans.

Munk returned to service for his king. During the Thirty Years War (1618-1648) he was commissioned Admiral, and he served on the Weser.

Quotes from Jens Munk:

-I gave the [sick] men wine and strong beer which they had to boil afresh, for it was frozen to the bottom.

-The peculiar illness (scurvy) caused great pains in the loins, as if a thousand knives had been thrust there. At the same time, the body was discolored as when someone has a black eye, and all the limbs were powerless, all the teeth were loose so that it was impossible to eat.

-As I could no longer stand the smell of the dead bodies that had remained on the ship so long, I managed to crawl out of my berth . . . I spent the night on deck, wrapped in the clothing of those who were already dead.[2]

---

1 "Enhiornigen" and "Lamprenen" in Danish.
2 Quoted in Peter C. Newman. *Company of Adventurers*. Markham: Penguin Books, 1985. pp 49-50.

OBERON

When you travel south from Neepawa on Highway #5, you will soon be in the Oberon district, whose citizens might say with pride that their community is the only one in the province whose name honors William Shakespeare: or at least one of the characters in his plays. You might be invited to the court of King Oberon and Queen Titania, or is that just a Midsummers Night's Dream? If someone offers to place love-juice on your eyelids, think twice before accepting. Puck will say to you, "Lord, what fools these mortals be!"

WILLIAM SHAKESPEARE (1564-1616)

Nearly all that has come down to us of the personal history of Shakespeare (there are many spellings of his name) may be expressed in the words of one of his biographers: "All that is known with any degree of certainty is, that he was born at Stratford-upon-Avon, married, and had children there, went to London, where he commenced acting and wrote poems  and plays and then returned to Stratford, made his will, and was buried."

Shakespeare left no records of his life. It is reported that his father, John, a glover and alderman, was a son of a prosperous farmer near Stratford. In 1557, John married Mary Arden, daughter of a landowner. Mary gave birth to a number of children. William Shakespeare was the third born. Perhaps young William received his early education at the Free Grammar School of Stratford, which he entered about age seven, and which he stayed at for six years or so. One tradition suggests that he was apprenticed to a butcher. Another places him as a schoolmaster for a short time. Some biographers claim that William became acquainted with strolling players-actors who occasionally visited Stratford. Somehow, he felt their influence.

Documentary evidence shows that William Shakespeare, at age eighteen, "hurriedly" married Anne Hathaway, some eights years his senior, on November 28, 1582. Their first child, Susana, was born in May 1583. Hammet and Judith, twins, were born in 1585. It has been suggested that Shakespeare showed little love for Anne, although he did return to their home after his success in London.

It appears that Shakespeare left for London in 1586-1587, where he became launched as an actor and playwright. Queen Elizabeth I was a great admirer of his plays. In his *Midsummer's Night's Dream,* he paid his Queen a most refined tribute:

> And the Imperial Votaress passed on
> In maiden meditation, fancy free.

Clearly, Shakespeare's pen led to his public acceptance, more so than his fine acting skills. He traveled the highway to considerable fame and wealth. For almost twenty years, he produced an average of two plays a year for the brilliant company of which he was a part. He owned a piece of the famous Globe theater, among others, where his works were presented. He owned London properties, and Stratford's second largest house.

William Shakespeare was buried on the north side of the chancel of Stratford Church. On a flat grave-stone, this inscription was made:

> Good friend, for Jesus sake, forbeare
> To dig the dust enclosed heare.
> Blese be ye man yt spares thes stones,
> And ovrst [curst] be he yt moves my bones.

Today, many people believe in that curse. Others want the remains to be dug from their resting place. They claim that Bacon or Marlowe, among others, wrote some or all of Shakespeare's plays. Those doubters are left without proof.

Shakespeare, who wrote at least thirty-eight plays and at least 154 sonnets, left the world thousand of memorable quotes. To appease citizens of the Oberon district, here are a few of the bard's quotations from *A Midsummer Night's Dream*, written in 1595 or 1596:

-The course of true love never did run smooth.

-Nay, faith, let me not play a woman, I have a beard coming.

-Hold, or cut bow-strings.

-The wisest aunt, telling the saddest tale.

-Ill met by moonlight, proud Titania.

-I'll put a girdle round about the earth in forty minutes.

-Look in the almanack; find out moonshine, find out moonshine.

-What angel wakes me from my flowery bed.

-Two lovely berries moulded on one stem;
So, with two seeming bodies, but one heart.

-Cupid is a knavish lad,
Thus to make poor females mad.

-The lunatic, the lover, and the poet,
Are of imagination all compact.

-The iron tongue of midnight hath told twelve;
Lovers, to bed; 'tis almost fairy time.

Shakespeare has had criticism from other great writers. Consider:

-The unquestionable glory of a great genius which Shakespeare enjoys is a great evil, as is every untruth.
                                        Leo Tolstoy.

-Shakespeare's plays are bad enough, but yours are even worse.
> Leo Tolstoy, to Anton Chekov.

-It would be a relief to dig him up and throw stones at him.
> George Bernard Shaw.

-I have tried lately to read Shakespeare, and found it so intolerably dull that it nauseated me.
> Charles Darwin, Evolutionist.

-A sycophant, a flatterer, a breaker of marriage vows, a whining and inconstant person.
> Elizabeth Forsyth, British writer.

-Crude, immoral, vulgar and senseless.
> Leo Tolstoy, Russian writer.

-This enormous dunghill.
> Voltaire, French writer and philosopher.

-Shakespeare – what trash are his works in gross.
> Edward Young, British poet.

-Shakespeare never had six lines together without a fault. Perhaps you may find seven, but this does not refute my general assertion.
> Dr. Samuel Johnson, critic, lexicographer, poet.

Image: A portrait of William Shakespeare attributed to a little-known artist named John Taylor, and dated by experts to between 1600 and 1610, the Chandos portrait provides an unusually bohemian image of Shakespeare, dressed in black, sporting a gold hoop earring and with the strings on his white collar rakishly untied. The portrait was shown on display at the National Portrait Gallery in London as part of an exhibition of portraits and manuscripts from Shakespeare's lifetime called *Searching for Shakespeare*.

OGILVIE

Travel a bit east of Neepawa and then turn north on Highway #260 to Ogilvie. Please survey the area carefully, just as the individual after whom the place was named would.

WILLIAM OGILVIE (1849-1912)

British presence on the Yukon River region began in 1840, when the HBC's Fort Frances was established. In 1870, the region became part of the North West Territories. The Yukon River region was then a kind of no-man's-land, where adventurers, miners, and trappers acted freely. During and just before the Yukon gold rush, the NWMP was sent there to keep order and to prevent a possible U.S. takeover via Alaska.

Commissioner William Ogilvie came to that region, and earned his reputation as an able, honest, and hardworking civil servant there during the 1898-1901 period. Ogilvie, an expert surveyor, plied his trade and expertise earlier surveying the Yukon-Alaska border. (The border was "finalized" in 1903, when the Alaska panhandle dispute was settled.) In 1896, Ogilvie surveyed the Klondike goldfield region and the town site of Dawson. It was his steady hand that made his efforts as Commissioner successful.

Ogilvie was elected a fellow of the prestigious Royal Geographical Society in recognition of his numerous and careful surveys in western Canada, including the Yukon.

The Ottawa-born Ogilvie was further honored in 1966 when a mountain range north of Dawson was named after him.

If a surveyor may be called a "person of the pen", then William Ogilvie surely qualifies (this book lists many surveyors after whom Manitoba place names were made. Perhaps Ogilvie's place in this book can represent all those surveyors' contributions).

Comments[1] about William Ogilvie:

-Few men were better fitted for the task of unsnarling the Klondike tangle, where the shifting of stakes by a few feet might mean the loss or gain of thousands of dollars. Ogilvie was as incorruptible as he was scrupulous.

-Here was a man with a sense of history . . . [the] sense of propriety had been an act of faith with Ogilvie.

---

1 Pierre Berton. *Klondike: The Last Great Gold Rush 1896-1899.* Toronto: McClelland & Stewart, 1972.

Pendennis

A bit northwest of Brandon, there was a railway point called Pendennis, named after the name of a novel by William Makepeace Thackeray, writer and public lecturer. If you meet a man there who has had numerous lovers – many unhappy – but who finally marries the right woman, then you'll know for sure you are in Pendennis area.

William Makepeace Thackeray (1811-1863)

William was born in India, where his father served the East India Company. When he was five, his father died. The lad was sent to England to be reared by an aunt, who enrolled him in the famous Charterhouse School. He had his nose badly broken in a fight there; that crooked beak was never straightened.

The youth tried Cambridge University, but did not take a degree. He then toured the continent, and tried law and journalism. While in a Parisian art school, he met and married a penniless Irish girl, Isabella Shawe. The Thackerays had three daughters before Isabella's "mental derangement" ended their marriage.

His successful work as a journalist, especially with *Punch*, encouraged him to become a full-time writer.

At age thirty-seven, Thackeray published the novel *Vanity Fair*, which brought him swift popularity, especially among the "upper classes", in spite of the fact it satirized them. His novel describes the roles of the scheming woman, Becky Sharp. Pretense, snobbery, pomposity, and sham, among other traits, angered the writer. (He claimed that "every person who manages another is a hypocrite.") He followed that success with *Pendennis* and *Henry Esmond*, a story about the reign of Queen Anne, and considered to be one of the best historical novels in the English language.

The author fell ill with cholera in 1849, when the novel *Pendennis* was only half-finished. When Thackeray later wrote the last part of the novel, he used a much more somber tone. Indeed, the character Pendennis had many of the same qualities and experiences as did the author.

Thackeray became a public lecturer, and made two lecture tours to the United States. His book *The Virginians* was set partly there. He created a rather favorable picture of the American south.

The somewhat bitter humorist was once asked about his smoking habit. He replied: "The pipe draws wisdom from the lips of the philosopher and shuts up the mouth of the foolish." However, friends considered Thackeray to be a kind, loveable, and open-minded individual. He was an impressive, tall man, with a large head and "a big body to match."

Thackeray became a candidate for Parliament, but was defeated.

The gifted writer also wrote verse and entertaining ballads. It seems that his hard work and long hours led to his bad health. Thackeray died two days before Christmas in 1863, in spite of the devoted care of his daughters. A commemorative bust of him was placed in Westminister Abbey.

The author blackballed a man proposed for membership in London's Garrick Club: "I blackballed him because he is a liar, he calls himself ill when he isn't." At that club, Thackeray was confronted by a pompous Guards officer who teased the writer because he was going to have his portrait painted. "Full-length?" asked the officer. Thackeray replied: "No, full-length portraits are for soldiers, so we can see their spurs. With authors, the other end of the man is the principal thing."

His bitter pen offered this negative assessment of Americans' lack of grace: "I saw five of them at supper . . . the other night with their knives down their throats. It was awful." Criticism flew both ways. British art critic and author John Ruskin commented: "Thackeray settled like a meat-fly on whatever one had for dinner; and made one sick of it."

However, as the following statement by Thackeray suggests, the writer also had his moments of self-deprecation: "Even when I am reading my lectures I often think to myself, what a humbug you are, and I wonder the people don't find it out." He was the same man who said, "I never know whether to pity or congratulate a man on coming to his senses."

Thackeray! A big man with a sharp pen! Observe:

-He who meanly admires mean things is a Snob.

-It is impossible, in our condition of Society, not to be sometimes a Snob.

-We love being in love, that's the truth on't.

-Nothing like blood, sir, in hosses, dawgs, and men.

-'Tis strange what a man may do, and the woman yet think him an angel.

-Why do they always put mud into coffee on board steamers? Why does the tea generally taste of boiled boots?

-When I say that I know women, I mean that I know that I don't know them. Every single woman I ever knew is a puzzle to me, as, I have no doubt, she is to herself.

-Remember, it is as easy to marry a rich woman as a poor woman.

-There are some meannesses which are too mean even for a man – woman, lovely woman alone, can venture to commit them.

-If a man's character is to be abused . . . there is nobody like a relation to the business.

-To inspire hopeless passion is my testing (*Pendennis*).

–The *Pall Mall Gazette* is written by gentlemen for gentlemen (*Pendennis*).

–Business first; pleasure afterwards.

Thackeray's pen could drip venom. Consider what he wrote about Jonathan Swift, British satirist and essayist: "A monster of gibbering shrieks, and gnashing imprecations against mankind tearing down all shreds of modesty, past all sense of manliness and shame; filthy in thought, furious, raging, obscene."

Rembrandt

Here is the guarantee: If you bring your brushes, paints, and other requirements to Rembrandt, a bit northwest of Gimli, and then you paint a masterpiece as great as the artist after whom that settlement is named could, you will become a very wealthy individual.

Rembrandt Harmenz van Rijn (1606-1669)

The baker's daughter married the miller and bore ten children. Their ninth child, a genius, has become known across the world.

The Leiden-born youth attended the Latin School before he attended Layden University. After working with other artists in Amsterdam, he returned to his home town. There, he excelled at group portraits of the burghers of Amsterdam.

In 1634, Rembrandt married Saskia van Ulenburgh, a well connected daughter of a burgomaster. Saskia, who bore him a son, Titus, was the subject of a number of Rembrandt's paintings.

Saskia died in 1642, the year that Rembrandt produced his most famous painting, *The Military Company of Captain Frans Banning Cocq* – better known as "The Night Watch" – a dramatically lit and dynamically composed group portrait of a local militia band.

As Rembrandt's fame increased, his finances declined over the next twenty-five years or so. He narrowly avoided bankruptcy at least once. After 1647, he lived with Hendricke Staffels, who bore him a daughter, Cornelia. She was featured in a number of Rembrandt's works. She and his son Titus took control of the artist's sales and finances.

Gradually, Rembrandt turned to biblical subjects. More group portraits also followed. Perhaps *de Staalmeesters* was the greatest of those works. He also did a marvelous series of self-portraits, plus ink-and-wash drawings, and etchings.

Experts contend that Rembrandt "reinvented" the media in which he worked. His technical mastery and a sense of drama permeates his paintings. It has been claimed that his self-portraits were the first psychological studies in the history of art.

The genius had an enormous output: over 600 paintings (including five dozen self-portraits), 2000 drawings, and nearly 300 etchings.

John Hunt (1775-1848), English art critic offered this dubious comment: "Rembrandt is not to be compared in the painting of character with our extraordinary [sic] gifted English artist, Mr. Rippingille."

Rennie

Visit Rennie, a settlement east of Winnipeg, and ask the locals what connection Rennie has with Lake Havasu City, Arizona. You might be told a story about a certain bridge, or you might be serenaded with the old song *London Bridge is Falling Down*.

John Rennie (1761-1821)

Rennie was the fourth son of a prosperous farmer, whose estate was twenty miles east of Edinburgh, Scotland. Young John was known to have "skipped school" to watch men work at the local millwright's workshop (owned by the inventor of the threshing machine, Andrew Meikle) where, at age twelve, he began to work when not in classes. Rennie studied at the University of Edinburgh; afterwards he worked for a farm that manufactured steam engines near Birmingham, England.

At age thirty, Rennie moved to London, where he established his own engineering business. His first endeavors there involved canals and drainage systems. His first large project was the Albion Flour Mills in London. It was the first British factory to be constructed entirely of cast iron. He made innovative use of machinery and methods in that project.

From 1804, Rennie worked on the construction of docks in London, Dublin, Hull, Liverpool, and Holyhead using cast iron and masonry. He also built docks for use by the Royal Navy.

The engineer became famous as a bridge builder. His busy pen produced plans and designs for bridges at Leeds, New Galloway, as well as Southwark and Waterloo, among others (his most famous works were a series of bridges across the Thames).

John Rennie's talents allowed him to improve harbors at Chatham, Sheerness, and Plymouth, where he constructed the famous breakwater. He was frequently asked for advice on other maritime structures such as steam-powered dredges, diving bells, and lighthouses.

It was John Rennie's pen that drew plans for London Bridge (1824-1831), which was completed by his son ten years after the elder Rennie died. That bridge was dismantled in 1970 and carefully reassembled in Arizona. Hence the connection with Manitoba's Rennie. Hence another way for tourists to rid themselves of money spent on bridge souvenirs, trinkets, postcards, and more.

John Rennie was buried in St. Paul's Cathedral. His sons followed their father's footsteps, becoming notable engineers. Rennie's notebooks, 1784-1813, are in the National Library of Scotland and in Edinburgh University Library. A man of the pen!

Note: Many of Rennie's bridge projects were closely tied to the new road network of fellow Scottish engineer Thomas Telford. (See Telford)

Riel

The locality of Riel is now part of St. Vital, which in turn is part of Greater Winnipeg. Riel was named in honor of the family of Louis Riel senior. Included, of course, is son Louis Riel, whose imprint on Canadian history is continuing to be evaluated. Many streets, roads, buildings, and parks are named in his honor.

Louis Riel (1844-1885)

This "founder of Manitoba," Métis leader, and central figure in two rebellion-resistances in western Canada continues to ignite controversy. Louis Riel was educated in St. Boniface and studied for the priesthood at the Collège de Montreal. In 1865, he studied law with Rodolphe Laflamme, and perhaps worked briefly in Chicago and St. Paul before returning to St. Boniface in 1868.

The introspective and religious Riel has had his biography "written" by historians, playwrights, poets, and movie makers. His part in the 1869-70 Manitoba rebellion and the 1885 Saskatchewan rebellion is well known by most Canadians. His diary and poetry make him a genuine Manitopen! After all, it was Riel, condemned prisoner, who wrote: "death waits for me as the inkwell waits for my pen."

In more recent years, Riel has become somewhat of a Canadian folk hero. One wonders why this man, hanged for his activities against Canada, has become such a central figure in the minds of Canadians. The murder of Thomas Scott, his alleged insanity, and his "martyrdom" continue to cause debate.

Riel's many defenders claim Riel to have been spokesman and symbol of the oppressed, a revolutionist, and a leader of a people. As one writer said: "Riel has gone from being a piece of western folklore to a symbol of western grievance."[1] The attachment of Riel to the concerns of French-English relations is real and strong. He has become a subject of fascination for countless Canadians, even though many rank Riel a failure as a military tactician (perhaps that role was too much to ask from a peace-loving individual).

Perhaps what must be remembered, in the classic tradition of heroes, is that Louis Riel died for his cause. One writer even called him "Canada's Joan of Arc."[2]

Some of Riel's thoughts follow:

-If ever, in time to come, we should have the misfortune to become divided – as foreigners have sought before – that will be the signal for all disasters which we have until now so happily avoided. But let us hope that the lessons of the past will guide us in the future!

Louis Riel, to the Nation of the Northwest, April, 1870.

-We must make Canada respect us.

Riel, telling why he would not stop the killing of Thomas Scott.

-I know that through the grace of God I am the founder of Manitoba.

Queen vs. Riel (trial), 1886, p. 147.

-The prophet of the New World.

Riel's description of himself.

-Politics will save me.

Riel after the Battle of Batoche.

-Tremble my heart, and bid my resound!
 Before you Peace displays a vaster field
 Than open countryside or battle ground.
 Before God's peace the grave cannot but yield.
 Amidst gigantic struggles, peace of mind
 Alone outweighs all other qualities.

-The man who has it certainly will find
  Defeats becoming mighty victories.
  I tell you, friends, 'tis only Jesus's peace
  Which fills our hearts with joy in every way.
  Though good, the blessings of this world soon cease
  To satisfy, and lead us far astray.
  Have peace of mind, and trust God to uncover
  New depths of joyous wisdom in your soul.
  With the peace of God, your eyes will soon discover
  Happiness – entire, whole!
  To do God's will lends us tranquility.
  It makes us calm when danger comes in view.
  Toward heaven lift your hands in humility
  Through the grace of God we can be born anew!
  Blessed Virgin, send down a flood of light
  To illuminate the human race.
  A river of prayers I ask through Joseph's might
  To save us today, and all our sins efface.
                    Riel's prison-written poem,
              August 1885, pp 105-6. Flanagan.

-Glory be to the Father, to the Son and to the Holy Spirit!
  As it was in the beginning, is now and ever shall be,
  world without end. Amen.
  Death hovers over me like a Great bird of prey flying over
  a chicken which it wants to carry off.
  Death keeps guard at the door of my cell.
  Death peers at me behind my prison bard.
  Death watches at my door like a Labrador retriever
  keeping watch in front of the house.
        Riel's prison diary for August 1885. P. 106. Flanagan.

-My God! I offer You through Jesus Christ my death sentence, my imprisonment, my chains, the weight of my chains, my privations, my pains, my sufferings. I join them to the passion of our beloved Savior that it may please You, because of His infinite merits, to pour out Your divine Spirit on all men and to renew the face of the earth.

-Save me with the help of the prayers of Mary and Saint Joseph. Dictate to me Yourself, O my God, the petition which I am writing now, through Jesus Christ.

Riel's written prayer for
August 23, 1885. p. 137. Flanagan.

-God wants the planet Venus to change its name and be called "Maria."
God wants the planet Mercury to be called "Anna."
God wants the planet Mars to be called "Julia."
God wants the planet Jupiter to be called "Marguerite-Marie."
God wants Neptune to be called "Catherine-Aurélie."
God wants the planet Uranus to be called "Josepha."
God wants the Big Dipper to be called the "Fabien Barnabé."
God wants the North Pole to be called "Henrietta.:
God wants the planet Saturn to be called "Sophia."
God wants the Morning Star to be called "Damase-Carrière."
God wants the galaxy to be called "the galaxy of the Grey Sisters." In everyday speech, when one refers to the galaxy, one should say, "the Grey Sisters."

Revelations in Riel's prison diary for
October 17-18, 1885. p. 164. Flanagan.
_{Note: the above names are those of Riel's
family, associate, relatives and friends.}

-Manitoba will become totally French-Canadian Métis. Five hundred years from now, her Métis population will number forty-million souls. And in her turn she will bear the name of the "House of Charlemagne."

Riel's diary, item for
October 17-18, 1885. p. 166. Flanagan.

-The Indians of the northern part of this continent are of Jewish origin. The Indians of the south of this continent are Egyptian.
>
> Riel's prison diary, item for October 17-18, 1885. p. 165. Flanagan.

-God wants Asia to be called "Xavieria" in honor of Saint Francois Xavier. God wants Africa to be called "Zabulonia" in honor of Zabulon, one of the children of Joseph. God wants Europe . . . to be called "Napoleonia" in honor of Napoleon . . ."
>
> Riel's diary item for October 17-18, 1885. p. 165. Flanagan.
> Note: Riel included many other items that he claimed were "revealed" to him by God.

Comments about Riel and his execution from *The Story of Louis Riel*:

-The Little Napoleon of Red River.
>
> A nickname.

-Strangle Riel with the French flag! That is the only use that rag can have in this country.
>
> *Toronto News,* May 18, 1885.

-He shall hang, though every dog in Quebec bark in his favor.
>
> Sir John A. Macdonald, 1885, to a friend who urged that Riel be shown mercy.

-Riel was fairly tried, honestly convicted, laudably condemned, and justly executed.
>
> *Winnipeg Free Press,* Dec. 17, 1885.

-It cannot be said that Riel was hanged on account of his opinions. It is equally true that he was not executed for anything connected with the late rebellion. He was hanged for Scott's murder; that is the simple truth of it.
>
> Sir Wilfred Laurier, letter to Blake, Dec. 31, 1885.

-Had there been no neglect there would have been no rebellion. If no rebellion, then no arrest. If no arrest, then no trial. If no trial, then no condemnation. If no condemnation, then no execution. They therefore who are responsible for the first are responsible for every link in that fatal chain.
> Edward Blake, on the execution of Riel, 1885.

-I do not propose to construct a political platform out of the Regina scaffold, or to create or cement party ties with the blood of the condemned.
> Edward Blake, speech in London, Jan. 14, 1886.

-Well, the God damned son of a bitch is gone at last.
> Comment by a NWMP member immediately after Riel was executed. Quoted in Joseph K. Howard. *Strange Empire*. Toronto: Swan, 1965, p. 470.

-Requiem mass was celebrated at St. Boniface on December 12 and the crowd of mourners overflowed into the churchyard and the street. Riel was buried in the peaceful, tree-shadowed cathedral yard.
> Howard, p. 472.

Louis Riel's Last Letter

Manitoba Pageant, September 1959, Volume 5, Number 1

On November 16, 1885 Louis Riel was hanged at Regina for his part in the North West Rebellion. The following letter was written to his mother the day before his execution. The original letter is in the Riel Collection in the Public Archives of Manitoba.

Prison de Regina, 15 Novembre 1885

Bien chère Maman,

J'ai reçu votre lettre avec votre sainte bénédiction. Hier matin, le Bon Pere André a attachée votre lettre au dessus de l'autel: et it a dit la sainte Messe pour moi, en action de grâce et en l'honneur de Marie Immaculée en me tenant pour ainsi dire lui même a l'ombre de votre benediction. Ce matin le Bon Père a pris la lettre de votre bénédiction; il me l'a mise sur la tête, au moment de la messe où comme célébrant, it donne la bénédiction; et c'est ainsi qu'unissant sa bénédiction a la vôtre, il a répandu sur moi les graces de la messe et l'abondance des biens spirituels et temporels que vous emplorez en ma faveur, en faveur de ma chere épouse, de mes chers petits enfants, de mes freres et soeurs bien-aimés, de mes beaux frères et belles soeurs chéris, de mes neveux et de mes nièces qui me sont tous très chers.

Chère Maman, que ma prière de fils-ainé, que mes voeux et mes prières de serviteur du Bon Dieu montent jusqu'à Notre Seigneur Jésus Christ, jusqu'au trône de Marie toujours Vierge et de Saint Joseph mon cher et grand protecteur; et que la misericorde, la consolation surabondante de Dieu, de tout ce que nous avons de cher et de plus cher dans le paradis descendent sur vous pour toujours.

Soyez bénie de généération en généération a cause de la grande bénédiction que vous avez versée sur moi et sur ma famille aussi bien que sur tous mes chers frères et soeurs, beaux frères et belles soeurs, neveux et nièces.

Soyez bénie de génération en génération pour avoir été bonne mère à mon ééard.

Que votre foi, votre espérance ferme et votre charité exemplaire soient comme des arbres chargés de fruits excellents, en présence de l'avenir. Et lorsqu'arrivera votre dernier jour, que le Bon Dieu soit tellement avec vous que votre pieuse esprit laisse la terre sur les ailes de l'amour des choses du ciel.

Il est deux heures après midi, le Bon Père André m'a dit ce matin de me tenir bien prêt pour demain. Je l'écoute, je lui obéis. Je me prépare à tout, selon son conseil et sa vive recommendation.

Mais le Bon Dieu m'aide à me tenir en paix et en doucer comme l'huile dans un vase que rien ne dérange.

Je fais tout ce que je peux pour me tenir prêt à tout événement en me conservant dans un calme inalterable suivant la pieuse exhortation du Vénére Archevêque Ignace Bourget.

Hier et aujourd'hui j'ai priéé Dieu de vous rassurer de bonne heure et de vous faire arriver à tous la consolation la plus douce afin que vos coeurs ne soient pas trop durement dans l'inquiétude et la souffrance.

Je vous embrasse tous avec la plus grande affection.

Vous chère Maman, je vous embrasse comme doit faire un fils don't l'âme est pleine d'amour filial.

Vous ma chère épouse, je vous embrasse comme doit le faire un époux chrétien, selon l'esprit catholique de l'union conjugale.

Mes chers petits enfants, je vous embrasse comme doit le faire un père chrétien, en vous bénissant selon l'etendue de la miséricorde divine, pour la vie présente et pour la vie future.

Vous mes chers freres, et soeurs, beaux freres et belles soeurs, neveux et nièces, parents, proches et amis, je vous embrasse avec tous les bons sentiments don't mon coeur est capable. Soyez-tous heureux - chère Maman,

Je suis votre fils affectueux soumis et obéissant.

Louis "David" Riel.

A photograph of the original letter in the Provincial Archives.
Source: The Manitoba Historical Society

---

1 Douglas Owram. "The Myth of Louis Riel." *The Prairie West: Historical Readings*. Edmonton: Pica Pica Press, 1985, p. 175.
Note: Readers searching for the historiography surrounding works on Riel should read Owram's article.
2 Hector Coutu. *Lagimodiére and their Descendants*. Edmonton: 1980, p. 63.
3 See Thomas Flanagan (ed.) *The Diaries of Louis Riel*. Edmonton: Hurtig Publishers, 1976.

Rudyard

Just west of Morden was a railway point once called Kaleida Junction. In Greek, Kaleida means "beautiful." When the literary giant Rudyard Kipling came to Canada in 1890, Kaleida's name changed to Rudyard in the writer's honor.

Rudyard Kipling (1865-1936)

The Bombay-born and English-educated Kipling was one of those rare writers equally at home in verse and in prose. At age seventeen, he returned to India, where he edited a newspaper. He was an acknowledged master of the short story by the age of twenty-five. His stories of the common soldier and sailor opened up a new literary field. Before long, he was considered "a poetic press agent" for the British Empire.

The English novelist, poet, and short-story writer is well remembered for his "celebration" of British imperialism and his stories for adults and children based in India and Burma. To this day, his stories for children – the *Jungle Books*, *Captains Courageous* (placed on Canada's Grand Banks), and *Just So Stories* – remain popular. In his early twenties, he traveled to Japan, China, and America. Writer Henry James was one of the first to feel "the irresistible magic of scorching suns, subject empires, uncanny religions, uneasy garrisons" in Kipling's tales. Kipling became famous for his "hard reality." *The Man Who Would Be King, Back Room Ballads*, and *Kim* are examples of his prose writing. In 1907, he won the Nobel Prize for Literature.

The low point in his life was when his teenage soldier-son was killed in World War I. It was Rudyard Kipling who, as a member of the War Graves Commission, suggested the standard inscription in the Stone of Sacrifice in each military cemetery of World War I: "their name liveth for evermore."

Countless students have memorized *Fuzzy-Wuzzy* and other Kipling poems. Millions more have sung his 1897 poem, *Recessional*, set to music:

> The tumult and the shouting dies;
> The Captains and the Kings depart:
> Still stands Thine ancient sacrifice
> An humble and a contrite heart.
> Lord God of Hosts be with us yet,
> Lest we forget—lest we forget!

Readers will recall other famous quotations and phrases from Kipling:

-Words are, of course, the most powerful drug used by mankind.

-You big black boundin' beggar – for you we broke the British square.

-You're a better man than I am, Gunga Din.

-The White Man's burden.

-A woman is only a woman, but a good cigar is a smoke.

-The female of the species is more deadly than the male.

-You may carve it on his tombstone, you may cut it on his card / That a young man married is a young man marred.

-Oh, East is East and West is West, and never the twain shall meet . . .

-The sin ye do by two and two ye must pay for one by one.

A favorite Kipling statement:

-The style of a man's play, plus the normal range of his vices, divided by the square of his work, and multiplied by the coefficient of his nationality, gives not only his potential resistance under breaking-strain but indicates, within a few points, how far he may be trusted to pull off a losing game.

Canadian soldiers today might reflect on Kipling's lines written about Britain's earlier military attempt to secure the Afghanistan region:

> When you're wounded and left on Afghanistan's plains,
> An' the women come to cut up what remains,
> Jest roll your rifle an' blow out your brains
> And go to your Gawd like a soldier.

(Kandahar, Saskatchewan, was named after the site of a famous battle won by the British army under Roberts during the Afghanistan War of 1879-1880).

Kipling had a keen edge to his pen. He wrote that "the American has no language. He has no dialect, slang, provincialism, accent, and so-forth." Kipling saved some of his sharper comments for Medicine Hat, Alberta: "You people in the district seem to have all Hell for a basement."

Kipling's 1897 *Our Lady of the Snows* described Canada's relations with Britain in terms of those of a daughter and a mother. The last verse is as follows:

> A Nation spoke to a Nation,
> A Throne sent word to a Throne,
> "Daughter am I in my mother's house,
> But mistress in my own.
> The gates of mine to open,
> As the gates are mine to close,
> And I abide in my Mother's House,"
> Said our Lady of the Snows.

Kipling also commented on Western Canada: "The prairie which is the High Veldt, plus Hope, Activity, and Reward."

A newspaper wrongly announced Kipling's death. His written response: "I've just read that I am dead. Don't forget to delete me from your list of subscribers." At the height of his success, Kipling received a letter from an autograph hunter, who enclosed one dollar in the belief that the great man charged a dollar per word. "Please send me a sample," requested the letter writer. Kipling wrote back: "Thanks."

His "imperialistic persuasions" grew less popular as time passed. Today, many people associate Kipling with the Victorian Age. A typical sharp criticism came from the Welsh poet Dylan Thomas: "Mr. Kipling . . . stands for everything in this cankered world which I would wish were otherwise." One wonders how many Manitoban students, among others, struggled through *Kim* and memorized the famous poem *If*. Kipling: A literary giant. It was he who wrote:

> I had six honest serving men,
> They taught me all I know;
> Their names were Where and What and When
> And Why and How and Who.

St. Boniface

St. Boniface, part of Greater Winnipeg, is named after a martyr, brutally killed.

St. Boniface (c. 672-754)

The gang killed the old man with swords and spears at Dokkum, West Friesland. It wasn't murder, they claimed, because according to the *Lex Frisionum*, they had the right to kill Boniface because he had destroyed their shrines. Saint Boniface (c 672-754), the English-born missionary and apostle to the Germans, was born Wyunfrith or Winfrid in Devon.

In 723, Boniface (the name was given to him by Pope Gregory III) cut down a holy oak tree that was dedicated to the Norse god Thor. People called upon Thor to strike him down, if the power were there. Nothing happened, so many of the locals were convinced that Boniface's Christianity must be the proper religion. The felling of Thor's Oak is usually regarded as the beginning of German Christianization. Thousands were baptized in the Frankish Empire. Boniface made at least three trips to Rome, which recognized his efforts as a missionary and apostle. Pope Gregory III named him Archbishop and Primate of all Germany.

Boniface has been called the father of our Christmas tree tradition "because he cut down the trees that then were thought to represent Christ's cross. Boniface claimed that there was only one holy tree: the Cross. Because he wrote the first Latin grammar produced in England among countless sermons, St. Boniface can be called a "person of the pen."

In July 1968, the St. Boniface Basilica burned to the ground. The destruction of the cathedral, with its impressive spires, saddened the community.

Less well known is the 1860 fire which destroyed the earlier St. Boniface Cathedral. That edifice was honored by the poet, John Greenleaf Whittier (1807-1892):

> The bells of the Roman mission
> That call from the turrets twain
> To the boatman on the river
> The hunter on the plain
> The voyageur smiles as he listens
> To the sound that grows apace,
> Well he knows the vesper ringing
> Of the bells of St. Boniface.

St. Boniface Cathedral (Painting by William Napier in 1858)

Sarto

Head south from Steinbach to Sarto, a settlement many claim was named in honor of Andrea del Sarto, whose genius might inspire you to put paint, brushes, and easel to work.

Andrea del Sarto (1486-1530)

Robert Browning's marvelous poem, *Andrea del Sarto*, tells of the gifted poet's love for and frustration with his beautiful wife, Lucrezia del Fede. In the poem, the artist speaks to his wife, explaining how his work takes so much time. She is impatient because a caller is waiting for her company.

But do not let us quarrel any more,
No, my Lucrezia; bear with me for once
I often am much wearier than you think
Again the Cousin's whistle! Go my love.

The painter's father was a tailor ("Sarto", in Italian) and the Florence-born genius derived his name from this fact. Andrea was likely initially trained by a goldsmith, but he later apprenticed with a painter and a creator of frescoes.

As a painter, Andrea chiefly painted religious subjects. In 1509, he was commissioned by the Servites to decorate their Cloisters of the Annunziata in Florence. His five frescoes there won him the title "the faultless painter."

The Florentine painter, equally famous for his frescoes and his oils, used sumptuous color and monumental composition in his work. His paintings consistently exemplify the High Renaissance ideal. Some of his works are: *Madonna in Glory, Madonna of the Harpies, Holy Family and Charity, Madonna and Child with St. John*, and many others.

Andrea del Sarto suffered a horrible death. On September 29, 1530, he died of the plague in Florence, Italy.

In 1568, biographer Vasari wrote of Andrea's "faultless works," but added "if Andrea had been somewhat bolder . . . he would have had . . . no equal . . . but a certain timidity, humility and simplicity in him never permitted that . . . " The earlier mentioned Browning poem reflects that opinion.

Selkirk

When you next visit Selkirk, a bit northeast of Winnipeg, ask the locals if they agree that Thomas Douglas Selkirk, after whom their town is named, should have a statue built in his honor-and have it placed in a beautiful local setting.[1]

Thomas Douglas Selkirk (1771-1820)

The 5th Earl of Selkirk was born at St. Mary's Isle, Kirkcudbrightshire. The youth witnessed the eviction of many Highlanders from their small holdings. He believed he had a solution to their problems: move them to Canada.

In 1803, the Scottish philanthropist founded a prosperous settlement in Prince Edward Island, and another at Baldoon in Upper Canada.

In 1811, Selkirk acquired a large area in Rupert's Land from the HBC (he had purchased a controlling interest in the company). In 1812, he sent out Scottish settlers to what became the Red River Settlement.

The Red River establishment led to bloodshed between the settlers and the North West Company, a rival of the HBC (see Hudson Bay). The NWC defeated Selkirk's interests in various legal proceedings.

Selkirk lost much of his fortune as a result of his generosity. His health declined sharply, and he died in France in 1820, a brokenhearted individual.

Earlier, Selkirk proved to be a man of the pen by writing *Observations on the Present State of the Highlands of Scotland* (1805) and *A Sketch of the British Fur Trade in North America* (1816).

Yes, locals who consider Selkirk "the Father of Manitoba" might well see to the creation of that statue in his honor.

After all, it was Lord Selkirk who wrote that "it is a very moderate calculation to say that if these regions were occupied by an industrious population, they might afford ample means of subsistence for 30 000 000 British subjects."

By the way, Brandon House was named in honor of the Duke of Brandon, an ancestor of Lord Selkirk.

---

1 Note: East Kildonan and West Kildonan, now part of Winnipeg, were also named by Selkirk in honor of parishes in Scotland. Kil is Celtic for church and Kildonan means St. Donan's church.

SHELLEY

On a warm summer day, bring your book of Shelly's poems, your favorite chair, and hours to spare to a certain locality a bit northeast of Winnipeg which was named in honor of a poetic genius. Read, relax, and reread. Time well spent!

PERCY BYSSHE SHELLEY (1792-1822)

At the last moment, Edward Trewlaney, a friend, reached into the flames and pulled Shelley's heart from the fire. The poet's body, among others, was cremated on an Italian beach two weeks after their boat went missing during a violent storm. The drowned Shelley had a volume of Keats in one pocket and a volume of Sophocles in another. Shelley's ashes were buried in Rome, and his heart was delivered to his wife, Mary.

Shelley, often considered to be the greatest English prophet of human perfectibility, a poet of protest against man's inhumanity to man, a great lyric poet who was also a perceptive social and political thinker, stressed the spirit of liberation and regeneration. Shelley's idealism motivated his attack on the world as he knew it, just as it inspired his hopes for a better world.

The Sussex-born Shelley was considered a trouble-maker at Eton and later at Oxford, where he read such skeptics as Hume, Locke, and Voltaire. The youth's writing attempted to demolish "evidence of Christianity." From Oxford, he was expelled because of his *The Necessity of Atheism*.

Shelley's love affairs and his writing led to a virtual sentence of exile from England. His poor health also led him to Italy in 1818. His career as an intellectual playboy was at an end. In Italy, he acquired a formidable circle of other clever writers and admirers, such as Lord Byron. The 1821 death of poet John Keats moved Shelley to write a poem in his honor.

Perhaps *Ozymandias* is Shelley's most famous poem. Others include *Hymn to Intellectual Beauty*, *Hymn of Pan*, *Song To The Men of England*, *Ode To The West Wind*, and *Love's Philosophy*. Major works include long visionary poems, such as *Adonais*, *The Revolt of Islam*, and *Prometheus Unbound*.

Although the term Romanticism has defied precise definition, the "movement" surely included Shelley, Wordsworth, Coleridge, and Byron. Many experts consider Shelley to be the finest of the Romantic poets. Author-clergyman Charles Kingsley called Shelley "a lewd vegetarian."

Readers will know that Shelley's wife Mary wrote *Frankenstein*, among other works of literature.

Quotes and Poems from Shelley:

-Thou Paradise of Exiles, Italy!

-His fine wit makes such a wound, the knife is lost in it.

-He hath awakened from the dream of life.

-From the great morning of the world when first God dawned on chaos.

-Chameleons feed on light and air:
  Poets' food is love and fame

-O, wind,
  If Winter comes, can Spring be far behind?

-Hell is a city much like London-
  A populous and smoky city.

-The wise want love; and those who know love
  want wisdom.

-To be omnipotent but friendless is to reign.

-How wonderful is Death,
  Death and his brother Sleep!

-A lovely lady, garneted in light
  From her own beauty.

-Monarchy is only the string that ties the robber's bundle.

-A widow bird sat mourning for love
  Upon a wintry bough.

-Hail to thee, blithe spirit!
  Bird thou never wert.

-O wild West Wind, thou breath of Autumn's being...

-As a bankrupt thief turns thief-taker in despair, so an unsuccessful author turns critic.

-Jealousy's eyes are green.

-Soul meets soul on lovers' lips.

OZYMANDIAS

I met a traveler from an antique land
Who said: "Two vast and trunkless legs of stone
Stand in the desert. Near them on the sand,
Half sunk, a shattered visage lies, whose frown
And wrinkled lip and sneer of cold command
Tell that its sculptor well those passions read
Which yet survive, stamped on these lifeless things,
The hand that mocked them and the heart that fed.
And on the pedestal these words appear:
"My name is Ozymandias, King of Kings:
Look on my works, ye mighty, and despair!"
Nothing beside remains. Round the decay
Of that colossal wreck, boundless and bare,
The lone and level sands stretch far away.

To Mary

O Mary dear, that you were here
With your brown eyes bright and clear.
And your sweet voice, like a bird
Singing live to its lone mate
In the ivy bower disconsolate;
Voice the sweetest ever heard!
And your brow more . . .
Than the . . . sky
Of this azure Italy,
Mary dear, come to me soon,
I am not well whilst thou art far;
As sunset to the sphered moon,
As twilight to the western star,
Thou, beloved, art to me.

O Mary dear, that you were here;
The Castle echo whispers 'Here!

Residents of the Shelley district might tell you the story of the poet Shelley and his "runaway bride." Miss Mary Godwin (author of "Frankenstein") had so much luggage that their donkey collapsed under its weight. So the young lady carried the luggage, and Shelley carried the donkey for a considerable distance.

STONEWALL

If you want to visit a centre named after a man (a pioneer postmaster) who in turn was named after a man, then a good choice would be Stonewall, a settlement a bit north of Winnipeg and a few cannon shots west of Selkirk.

THOMAS JONATHON "STONEWALL" JACKSON (1824-1863)

Perhaps next to Robert E. Lee, Thomas J. Jackson remains the most respected and revered of all Confederate commanders.

In 1851, the West Virginia-born Jackson became general professor at the Virginia Military Institute. The West Point graduate (1846) had earlier served with distinction as an artillery officer in the Mexican War.

When the Civil War (1861-65) started, Jackson, then a Colonel, was dispatched to Harper's Ferry. Then his brigade moved to Manassas to join Beauregard. There, he and his brigade were dubbed "Stonewall", because of their fighting spirit displayed at the first battle at Bull Run. Promotions had raised his rank to Major General.

The religious Jackson always regretted having to fight on Sundays. He was not always a successful general, and he lost his share of Civil War battles. However, some military historians consider him to be one of the most gifted tactical commanders in U.S. history. His leadership and planning for the Chancellorsville battle are still studied today. His innovations and boldness continue to inspire.

After the Chancellorsville battle, he was returning to his lines after reconnoitering the area. He was then shot and badly wounded by some of his own men. After his arm was amputated, he died eight days later on May 10, 1863, from pneumonia.

As Jackson lay dying, General Robert E. Lee said, "He has lost his left arm; I have lost my right." Stonewall Jackson's grave is in Lexington, Virginia.

The military man (and ex-professor) Jackson must also be considered a man of the pen. His careful, detailed maps and written tactics make that very clear, indeed.

It was he who said, "My duty is to obey orders." Jackson wrote: "Always mystify, mislead, and surprise the enemy, if possible."

At the Battle of Bull Run on July 21, 1861, General Elliott Bee glanced to the side and said: "There is Jackson with his Virginians standing like a stone wall, let us determine to die here, and we will conquer."

The last and dying words of Stonewall Jackson: "Let us cross over the river and rest under the shade of trees."

> Now Stonewall Jackson is a man worth taking an interest in. Few people in history have achieved greater fame in a shorter time period with less useful activity in the brainbox than Gen. Thomas J. Jackson. His idiosyncrasies were legendary. He was hopelessly, but inventively, hypochondrical . . . More than once her fell asleep at the dinner table with food in his mouth. ... [once] his lieutenants found it all but impossible to rouse him and lifted him, insensible, onto his horse, where he continued to slumber while shells exploded around him . . . He was given that nickname not for gallantry and daring but for standing inert, like a stone wall . . . he was just thirty-nine.[1]

---

1 Bill Gryson. *A Walk in the Woods*. Toronto: Doubleday, 1999. pp.178-179.

St. Vital

The parish and municipality of St. Vital, now part of Greater Winnipeg, is named in honor of the Rev. Vital-Justin Grandin.

Vital-Justin Grandin (1829-1902)

The pioneer priest was born in Saint-Pierre-la-Coeur, France, to Jean and Marie Veillard. He was a sickly child whose speech impediment and poor health lasted all his life.

Grandin completed his formal education at the Oblates of Mary Immaculate-run Grand Séminaire, April, 1864. A month later, he was sent overseas as a missionary to the Canadian northwest. Archbishop Taché had visited France in 1852, and had enthused the young Grandin about the challenges in western Canada.

The young priest reported to St. Boniface, was sent to a mission at Fort Chipewyan, Alberta, and later to the mission at Ile-à-la Crosse, Saskatchewan. He also visited missions in the far north and west.[1] In 1857, Grandin was named coadjutor bishop of St. Boniface, which meant that he would assist Bishop Taché in the administration of the massive parish that included most of the northwest.

At Taché's request, the huge parish was divided in 1869, creating the vicariate of Saskatchewan. Grandin, the pioneering Oblate missionary, became the first bishop to the newly created diocese. Bishop Grandin spent the rest of his life at St. Albert, northwest of Edmonton.

In 1875, Bishop Grandin lobbied the federal government for funding to aid health care, agriculture, and education for the west. Although he was a tireless advocate for the advancement of native and Métis, he was strong in his opposition to the ideas of Louis Riel. He advocated moderation and obedience instead.

Despite his poor health, Bishop Grandin remained devoted to his church, his work as an administrator and as a man-of-the-pen. He oversaw the construction of new schools, orphanages, hospitals, and a seminary. He also made trips to Europe to recruit new priests for western Canada. He was a tireless letter writer, but far too often, he felt, Ottawa ignored many of his pleas.

Bishop Vital-Justin Grandin's cause for sainthood was introduced in Rome in 1937.

Critics of Bishop Grandin suggest that he had a "distaste" for Indians, and that the Métis of Red River should be replaced by French farmers because "the Métis are careless people." The critics' position is difficult to defend.

---

1 The Districts of Athabaska, Alberta, Assiniboia, and Saskatchewan were formed in 1882.

2 An earlier pioneer clergyman, Joseph-Norbert Provencher (1787-1853) should be noted here. The Quebec-born bishop of St. Boniface (1847) was earlier sent to the troubled Red River colony in 1818 to build its first Catholic church. The 6'4" Provencher, a modest but uncompromising man, had deep suspicions about Protestantism. Education of the young, Catholic immigration, and conversion of Indians were some of his goals. He was appointed a bishop and apostolic vicar of the Northwest in 1820. Bishop Provencher is mentioned here given that his lengthy correspondence has been published in recent years. Schools, a bridge, and a Boulevard have been named in his honor, but no Manitoba settlement has been named for him.

Telford

Travel north and east from Winnipeg on Highway #44 to Whitemouth, where you will receive directions to the nearby community of Telford, named in honor of a famous Scottish engineer.

Thomas Telford (1757-1834)

Telford had a difficult childhood. He was born to a poor shepherd family at Westerkirk, Dumfriesshire, Scotland. Soon after the boy's birth, his father died. Young Thomas herded cattle to earn money for his family. After a basic education, he became very enthused about poetry, drawing, and chemistry. At age fourteen, he was apprenticed to a stonemason.

The young Telford traveled the country looking for work. In 1782, he arrived in London, and then found work at the Portsmouth dockyard. In 1797, Telford obtained the position of surveyor of public works in Shropshire from a Dumfries patron. His reputation was enhanced by his masonry arch bridge over the Severn River at Montford. His work on canals and aqueducts also met with approval; the Caledonian canal was perhaps the best of its kind. He built more than 1000 miles of road, numerous harbors, churches, manses, and nearly 1200 bridges. His road from London to Holyhead (and its 579 foot wrought-iron Menai Suspension Bridge) was a remarkable achievement. He also built the St. Katherine's Docks in London. Telford earned his nickname: "the Collosus of Roads." He built Edinburgh's Dean Bridge, and Sweden's Gotha Canal.

Telford often collaborated with the fellow Scot engineer John Rennie (see Rennie)[1]

The famous writer and poet Sir Walter Scott claimed that Telford's aqueduct at Point Cysylite was "the most impressive work of art I have ever seen."

Telford helped to form the Institute of Civil Engineers, and became its first president.

He was always ready with a humorous story or joke. Even though he was known as the finest civil engineer of his day, his suspension bridges made him nervous. On the days when the chains were to take the strain, Telford could be seen kneeling in prayer. Often, he took on projects for which he was not paid. He was not a rich man.

Thomas Telford was buried in Westminster Abbey.

Edinburgh's Telford College is named in his honor. So are Telford, Pennsylvania, and Telford, England.

Telford's ten volumes of papers describing his many projects are in the National Library of Scotland.

---

[1] The Telford community and the settlement of Rennie, both named after Scottish engineers, are "neighbors" east of Winnipeg.

Tipperary

With a song in your heart, drive northwest from Winnipeg on Highway #6 to Lundar in the Interlake region. There, inquire as to the way to the Tipperary district (it's not a long way to go!), where you and you your friends might begin your songfest with that song, made famous during World War I. The name Tipperary has been rescinded, but the melody lingers on.

The Song

Jack Judge (1872-1938) accepted the bet for five shillings, the price of a bottle of whiskey and almost a hundred cigarettes. The bet was that he could not write a song and then perform it during his next show. That late evening of January 30, 1912, the music-hall entertainer and composer had left "the Grand" in Stalybridge, England after his performance, wondering about his liquid-sponsored bet. He headed for a nearby club at about 1 a.m. From there – after a few drinks – he left for home. Along the way, he overheard a conversation between two men. One man, in response to a question said: "It's a long way to . . ."

Judge was taken by that response, and for some reason added Tipperary to it. Then the tired man slept on it. After his late morning breakfast of fresh fish, he went to a bar and wrote the music and words to "It's a Long Way to Tipperary." He won the bet!

The song became very popular, thanks in part to singer Florrie Forde, a popular music-hall songstress. Jack Judge made a small fortune from the royalties.

The song was adopted by the British army's 7th Battalion of the Connaught Rangers, and was played in march time. From World War I battlefields, the song spread world wide.

The song was reprinted many times.

One later sheet music cover described the song as "the Marching Anthem on the Battlefields of Europe."

VERSE 1:
Up to mighty London came an Irishman one day,
As the streets are paved with gold, sure ev'ryone was gay;
Singing songs of Piccadilly, Strand, and Leicester Square,
"Til Paddy got excited, then he shouted to them there:

CHORUS:
It's a long way to Tipperary, it's a long way to go;
It's a long way to Tipperary, to the sweetest girl I know;
Good-bye Piccadilly, farewell Leicester Square,
It's a long, long way to Tipperary,
but my heart's right there.

VERSE 2:
Paddy wrote a letter to his Irish Molly O',
Saying, "Should you not receive it, write and let me know!
If I make mistakes in spelling, Molly, dear," said he,
"Remember it's the pen that's bad,
don't lay the blame on me."

CHORUS:
It's a long way to Tipperary, it's a long way to go;
It's a long way to Tipperary, to the sweetest girl I know;
Good-bye Piccadilly, farewell Leicester Square,
It's a long, long way to Tipperary,
but my heart's right there.

VERSE 3:
Molly wrote a neat reply to Irish Paddy O',
Saying, "Mike Maloney wants to marry me, and so
Leave the Strand and Piccadilly, or you'll be to blame,
For love has fairly drove me silly, hoping you're the same."

CHORUS:
It's a long way to Tipperary, it's a long way to go;
It's a long way to Tipperary, to the sweetest girl I know;
Good-bye Piccadilly, farewell Leicester Square,
It's a long, long way to Tipperary,
but my heart's right there.

Tolstoi

Travel south on Highway 15, and before you reach the Canadian-American border you'll be in Tolstoi, named in honor of one of the world's greatest persons-of-the-pen. The settlement's earlier name (before 1910) was Oleskow, named for the man who encouraged Russian settlers from Tolstoi's estate to come to western Canada.

Leo Tolstoy[1] (1828-1910)

Count Leo Nikolayevich, religious philosopher and literary giant, was born at Yasnaya Polyana, an estate of his noble family in central Russia. He was educated privately before he read law and oriental languages at Kazan University. He did not graduate, but rather returned home to his family's estate. He spent his youth like some other nobles did in "dissipated pleasures", and later in army service. He published his earliest works, *Childhood* (1852), *Boyhood* (1854) and *Youth* (1857), a remarkable trilogy.

Tolstoy received a commission when he served during the 1854-56 Crimean War. He commanded a battery during the defense of Sebastopol. The horrors of war inspired him to write *Tales of Army Life,* which led him to the literary circles of St. Petersburg. He married Sophie Behrs in 1862. (They raised a family of thirteen children.)

His family settled on his Volga estate, and he devoted himself to the duties of a progressive landlord. There, he wrote *War and Peace*, an epic and domestic story, a depiction of Russian struggle, defeat, and victory over the forces of Napoleon Bonaparte, all set against the fortunes of certain noble families. (The book is considered by many people to be the greatest novel ever written.)

Tolstoy's second great literary effort, *Anna Karenina*, (1874-76) tells of the passion felt by a married woman for a young army officer, and her tragic fate. Other books followed: *The Death of Ivan Ilyich, Master and Man, the Cossacks, What I Believe*, and *What Men Live By*, among others.

From about 1880, Tolstoy's constant concern with moral questions developed into a crisis, which in turn led to radical changes in his life and writing. His moral position – including the renunciation of property, the abolition of churches and governments, non-resistance to evil, but a belief in God and a love for mankind – led to many of his works to be censored. In 1901, he was excommunicated by the Orthodox Church. However, his beliefs brought him a kind of morality, a large following, and his estate became a place of pilgrimage. (Today, Tolstoy's belief in non-violence and the simple life has many supporters. His works dealing with religion, moral aesthetics, and ethics continue to inspire.)

After one of his many domestic quarrels with his wife, he sought refuge by fleeing from his home with one daughter and his physician. He died of pneumonia in a siding of the Astapovo railway station, refusing to the last to see his waiting wife.

Leo Tolstoy, the consummate master of the psychological novel, has had his works translated into many languages and turned into movies.

Some of Tolstoy's better known comments include:

-All happy families resemble each other, each unhappy family is unhappy in its own way.

-Pure and complete sorrow is as impossible as pure and complete joy.

-Art is not a handicraft, it is the transmission of feeling the artist has experienced.

-There are no conditions of life to which a man cannot get accustomed, especially if he sees them accepted by everyone about him.

-All newspaper and journalistic activity is an intellectual brothel from which there is no retreat.

-The hero of my tale – whom I love with all the power of my soul, whom I have tried to portray in all his beauty, who has been, is, and will be beautiful – is Truth.

-History is nothing but a collection of fables and useless trifles, cluttered up with a mass of unnecessary figures and proper names.

-It is easier to produce ten volumes of philosophical writing than to put one principle into practice.

-There are many faiths, but the spirit is one, in me, in you, and in every man.

-A writer is dear and necessary for us only in the measure in which he reveals to us the inner working of his soul.

-Government is an association of men who do violence to the rest of us.

-Women are well aware that what is commonly called sublime and poetical love depends not upon moral qualities, but on frequent meetings, and on the style in which the hair is done up, and on the color and the cut of the dress.

Let Ernest Hemingway have the last word:

"I want to be the Champion of the World, but I have that son of a bitch Tolstoy blocking me and when I get by him I run into Shakespeare."

---

1 "Tolstoy" is a variant spelling of "Tolstoi", owing to the difficulty in transliterating between the Cyrillic and Roman alphabets.

Tremandan

This railway point, a bit northeast of The Pas, is named after a writer who admired the Métis culture. He would be pleased to learn that you proudly arrived by snowshoes. How fluent is your French?

Auguste-Henri de Trémandan (1874-1929)

Some experts claim that the strongly opinionated Trémandan was born in France, while others say he was Quebec-born. It is clear, however, that he was educated in France before he moved to western Canada. He studied law, and was called to the bar before moving to The Pas, where he and his uncle established a business. Trémandan edited a local newspaper called *Hudson Bay Herald*, later called *The Pas Herald*.

When Trémandan moved to St. Boniface, he made his first contact with the French-speaking l'Union Nationale Métisse, whose cause interested him greatly. That cause became his, and he spent the rest of his years defending it, i.e., the preservation of the French language in Manitoba.

For over fifteen years, Trémandan gathered materials used in the writing of his books. In 1924, health problems forced him to leave Manitoba for sunny California. With him, he took almost 300 volumes and a mass of documents, eyewitness statements, letters, and related materials.

Because of financial difficulties Trémandan, sold those sources to L'Union Nationale Métisse.[1] That organization then asked him to write *The History of the Métis Nation in Western Canada*. So he made use of those materials after all.

The book was not well received or reviewed in many quarters. Proofreading problems, lack of footnotes, historical inaccuracies, wrong dates and the like were noted. The book praised the use of French in Manitoba, and it displayed strong support for Riel's role in the Manitoba Resistance of 1869-70, and for his efforts during the 1885 Resistance-Rebellion in Saskatchewan.

Historian Trémandan scorned those responsible for the execution of Louis Riel.

His other works include *The Hudson Bay Road, Pourquoi, Nous Parlons Français, Petit Baptiste, Jesus Christ et la Famille, Le Sanq Français, Riel et la Naissance du Manitoba,* among others.

The Manitopen had an important part in the historography of Manitoba.

Comments from A.H. Trémandan:[2]

-From all points of view, therefore, the creation of a French province [Manitoba] would have been beneficial.

-If there is none more Catholic than a Métis there is none more French.

-So the Métis led a peaceful and happy life. Distress did not touch them except in cases of illness or idleness. The less fortunate could always count on help from their neighbors. Family life was respected, morals were of high standards, honesty and charity were a religion . . . but old-time Métis were also fond of fun and merriment.

-The Métis had a veneration for the missionaries that never watered. In their eyes the priest was indeed God's representative on earth.

-For having given in to the clamor of a band of insincere and lawless fanatics and for having allowed the execution of a patriot and a great heart [Louis Riel], when it would have been so easy and so noble to have pardoned him, Canada and England bear a stain of ignominy that will never be erased.

-The history of the Métis in the Canadian North West is worthy of a place in the glorious annals of the history of the world.

---

1 By 1909, old friends and associates of Louis Riel joined to form the Union Nationale Métisse St. Joseph de Manitoba. Their collection of anecdotes, memoirs, and memories of the events of 1869-70 led to Trémandon's writing of the Métis history.

2 Quotes are from Maquet's translation of *Hold High Your Heads.* Trémandan's title was *Histoire de la Nation Métisse.* See bibliography.

Tyndall

Southeast of Selkirk is the village of Tyndall, named in honor of a scientist who had the ability to discuss his disciplines with clarity and sureness. His remarkable discoveries only added luster to his name.

John Tyndall (1820-1893)

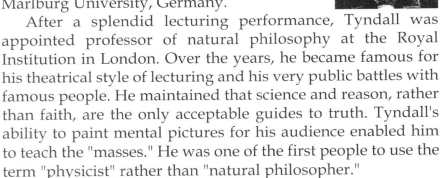

The Irish-born physicist, geologist, mathematician, draftsman, mountaineer, surveyor, and public lecturer was first employed as a railway engineer and surveyor before studying physics in England and at Marlburg University, Germany.

After a splendid lecturing performance, Tyndall was appointed professor of natural philosophy at the Royal Institution in London. Over the years, he became famous for his theatrical style of lecturing and his very public battles with famous people. He maintained that science and reason, rather than faith, are the only acceptable guides to truth. Tyndall's ability to paint mental pictures for his audience enabled him to teach the "masses." He was one of the first people to use the term "physicist" rather than "natural philosopher."

In 1856, Tyndall and T.H. Huxley made their first ascent of the Weisshorn, part of the Alps. Their studies of glaciers resulted in *The Glaciers of the Alps* in 1860. His research into radiant heat and the acoustic properties of the atmosphere led, in part, to the discovery of the "Tyndall Effect," the scattering of light by particles in solution which makes the light beam visible when viewed from the side. He also explained why the sky is blue.

Physicists today can explain the Tyndall Effect, the Tyndall Scattering, The Tyndall Cone, the Tyndello-meter, and Tyndallisation, all signs of Tyndall's genius.

Tyndall was also an early supporter of Louis Pasteur's germ theory of disease.

Today, John Tyndall is perhaps best remembered for his popularization and professionalism of science. He received five honorary degrees and membership in thirty-five scientific societies.

The great man died from an overdose of chloral hydrate administered in error by his wife.

Here are comments and thoughts from John Tyndall:

-Knowledge once gained casts a light beyond its own immediate boundaries.

-The formation of right habits is essential to your permanent security. They diminish your chance of falling when assaulted, and they augment your chance of recovery when over.

-The brightest flashes in the world of thought are incomplete until they have been proven to have their counterparts in the world of facts.

-Life is a wave which in no two consecutive moments of existence is composed of the same particles.

-The mind is a musical instrument with a certain range of tones, beyond which in both directions we have an infinite silence.

-Without water vapor, the Earth's surface would be held fast in the iron grip of frost.

To Manitobans, the community of Tyndall is known for Tyndall Stone, a unique building of Ordovician limestone, which was called Tyndall Stone after Sir John Tyndall, who first discovered the Devonian strata in the Welsh Hills was a similar deposition to the beds at Tyndall and Garson.

Because of its characteristic decorative mottling "like frost ferns on a window pane," Tyndall Stone is unique among building limestone, and as a result, the stone is sometimes called the "tapestry stone." The fossil content of stone is used for assigning geological age, and throughout Tyndall Stone there are many interesting fossils of ancient marine life.

Tyndall Stone enjoys a continent wide popularity. It was first used in the construction of Lower Fort Garry in 1832, just north of where Winnipeg now stands. Still standing as a testament to the durability of this stone are St. Andrews Anglican Church (see photo below), the oldest active stone church in western Canada, built in 1845, and the Captain Kennedy House, built in 1865. Other projects of significant profile that use Manitoba Tyndall Stone include the Manitoba Provincial Legislative Building, The Parliament Buildings in Ottawa, the Canadian Museum of Civilization in Hull, the Empress Hotel in Victoria, the Lied Centre for the Performing Arts in Omaha, and the Walsh Centre for the Performing Arts at the Texas Christian University campus in Fort Worth Texas.

St. Andrews Anglican Church (c. 1858)
Photographed by Humphrey Lloyd Hime, (1833-1903)
From Provincial Archives of Manitoba, *Manitoba Pageant*,
Spring 1967, Vol. 12, No. 3

Tyrrell

On the CNR line from The Pas to Churchill you'll find Tyrrell, named after a man whose long life was filled with hard work and dedication.

Joseph Burr Tyrrell (1858-1957)

After nearly a century of living, Joseph Burr Tyrrell, explorer, geologist, map maker, historian and mining expert could reflect on his life of accomplishment and contribution. In the process, he became a rather wealthy individual.

Tyrrell, born in Weston, Ontario, contracted scarlet fever which, permanently impaired his hearing. He was educated at Weston High School and Upper Canada College. After graduating in Arts from the University of Toronto in 1881, he began work with the Canadian Geological Survey. His doctor advised him to work outdoors.

In 1883, Tyrrell went on his first expedition to explore western Canada, then still unmapped in many areas. The following year, he led an expedition covering over 116 000 square kilomatres of Alberta in what is now called the Badlands. Then Tyrrell discovered coal deposits, and a fantastic collection of dinosaur bones.

Tyrrell explored the vast areas of northern and western Canada during his sventeen-year stint with the Geological Survey of Canada, confirming and correcting information collected by earlier explorers. He added knowledge to the ornithology, entomology, botany, geography, and mammalogy of the west and north of Canada.

In 1893, he served on an expedition across the Barren Lands from Lake Athabaska to Hudson's Bay, through northern Manitoba to Winnipeg. The 5150 km trip by dogsled and snowshoes (2 655 km had not been surveyed earlier) was a remarkable achievement.

Later, Tyrrell became a mining consultant, and then a miner in the Klondike. Considerable wealth came his way.

Tyrrell was also a man of the pen. He edited the diaries of Samuel Hearne and David Thompson. He was elected President of the Champlain Society. He was the recipient of many honors, including the RSC's Flavelle Gold Medal. His published reports and papers on his explorations make him a "fine reading experience."

In addition to the above noted Manitoba settlement, an Alberta Lake and mountain bear his name. The Tyrrell Museum of Paleontology at Drumheller, Alberta, continues to astound countless visitors. Many of Tyrrell's papers are in the University of Toronto Library.

Here are comments from and about Tyrrell:

-What the buffalo was to the North American Indian in days gone by, the reindeer is now to the Eskimos and other natives of the north country.

-The valleys and hillsides for miles appeared to be moving masses of caribou. To estimate their number would be impossible. They could only be reckoned [in 1897] in acres or square miles.

-He was the greatest land geographer the British race has provided.

> Tyrrell on David Thompson (1911).

-In the next century Canada may be expected to assume a somewhat similar position to that occupied by the United States in the last.

> Tyrrell in Yukon "Daily News," Jan. 1, 1901.

-The rocks proved to be rather interesting.

> Tyrrell on formations that produced the mining success of Flin Flon and Thompson.

Image: J.B. Tyrrell, 1886. University of Toronto, Fisher Rare Book Library MS Collection 26, Box 282

Note: Other "movers and shakers" have been honored by having Manitoba settlements named after them. Consider Cecil Rhodes (Rhodes is a railway point northeast of Killarney) and Lord Strathcona (Transcona is in the eastern part of Winnipeg), among others.

WALLACE LAKE

Near the Manitoba-Ontario border and north of Wadhope, you'll find Wallace Lake, named in honor of a distinguished Canadian university administrator.

ROBERT CHARLES WALLACE (1881-1955)

Manitoba, Alberta, and Ontario all rightly claim that the Scot-born Wallace brilliantly served those provinces and all of Canada.

Dr. Wallace graduated from universities in Edinburgh and Gottingen, Germany. Shortly after receiving his Ph.D. in geology in 1912, he married the remarkable Elizabeth Harcus Smith, also born in the Orkney Islands. That year, the couple moved to Canada, where Wallace became head of the Geology and Mineralogy department at the University of Manitoba. The erudite and charismatic Wallace was highly regarded by his students and colleagues.

Elizabeth Wallace – often called the best thing Dr. Wallace brought to Manitoba – later became founder and first president of the Faculty Women's Club at Queen's University.

During Wallace's sixteen years in Winnipeg, he also became Commissioner of Northern Manitoba, as requested by the provincial government. By canoe, dogsled, and foot, Wallace traveled northern Manitoba, documenting the extensive natural resources of the region. Later, he was promoted to the position of Commissioner of Mines.

The University of Alberta offered Wallace the Presidency in 1928. During the Depression, he helped to found a School of Nursing, and the now-called Banff School of Fine Arts. His fine speeches and decisiveness endeared him to the university in Edmonton.

Queen's University in Kingston, Ontario, beckoned in 1936. There, he again maintained that great teachers and researchers make for a great university. For many people, Wallace was the "voice" of Canadian universities. Wallace strongly supported the concept of academic freedom. He received honorary degrees from twenty universities. He retired from Queens in 1951, and then served as the head of the Arctic Institute of North America (1951-1955).

Memorable quotes from Dr. Wallace include:

-The critical test of the value of our educational systems is the attitude of adults to their own mental health.

-It is almost with a sense of shock that we realize that the essence of physics and chemistry alike lies in the arrangements within the atom.

-A dull teacher, with no enthusiasm in his own subject, commits the unpardonable sin.

WILLARD

At Willard, a former railway point south of Winnipeg, there is no statue or plaque which would honor a tireless, brilliant and well-loved woman named Frances Elizabeth Caroline Willard after whom the point was named. Should there be?

FRANCES WILLARD (1839-1898)

Willard – writer, editor, speaker, temperance reformer, educator and women's suffragist – proclaimed her beliefs with an average of 400 lectures per year over a ten-year period. Prohibition and votes for women were of deep concern for her, as she traveled over 30 000 miles per year in that same time period. The Churchville, New York-born Willard was elected president of the United States Women's Christian Temperance Union in 1879, a role she performed to the end of her life. She formed the worldwide W.C.T.U. in 1883, and was elected its president in 1888. As an academic, she became national president of Alpha Phi in 1887, and became the first dean of women at Northwestern University. In 1940, she was portrayed on a U.S. postage stamp.

Willard founded *The Union Signal,* a magazine. She wrote *A Great Mother, Glimpses of Fifty Years,* and dozens of magazine articles.

Willard was often called the "best loved woman in America." Carrie C. Catt, P. Beta Phi said of her, "There has never been a woman leader in this country greater than nor perhaps so great as Frances Willard." The famous writer John Greenleaf Whittier wrote of her: "She knew the power of bonded will, but felt the love was stronger still. And organized for doing good, the world's united womanhood."

While preparing to travel to England, Willard died in New York City. Biographer Ruth Bordin wrote this about Frances Willard: "No woman before or since was so clearly on the day of her death this country's (USA) most honored woman." [1]

The last comment belongs to Willard, who regretted her loss of energy in later years: "I'm like a dog that has lost its bone. Work was my bone and a meaty one it has been."

---

[1] Ruth Bordin. *Frances Willard: A Biography.* Chapel Hill: UNC Press, 1986, p. 280.

Part II

Manitoba Trivia

A. Manitoba Abundant and Beautiful

If you were a visitor from afar, what would you think when you learned that Manitoba's beauty and abundance were celebrated in such place names as Beautiful Plains (today's Arden), Altbergthal (old mountain vale in German), Belair (belle for beautiful and aire for area), Fredensthal (peaceful valley in German), Clematis, Eden, Edenburg, Friedensruh (tranquil rest of Mennonite origin), Gardenton, Garland, Gimli (the Great Hall of Heaven in Icelandic), Goodlands, Gnadenfeld (field of grass of Mennonite origin), Grodenthal (vale of grass of Mennonite origin), Grandview, Grand Beach, Grunthal (verdant vale in German), Hochstadt (lofty town in German), Ideal, Kaleida (beautiful in Greek; today's Rudyard), Kleefeld (cloven field in German), Kwesitchewan (glittering waters in Cree), Lily Bay, Lily Pad Lake, Miniota (water-plenty in Sioux), Minnedosa (flowing water in Sioux), Neepawa (abundance in Chippewa), Beautiful Plains (today's Oberon), Okno (refers to a new light in a new world in Russian), Pineimuta (partridge crop in Cree), Pheasant Point, Prawda (English spelling of the Ukrainian Pravda, meaning truth), Sans Souci (carefree in French), Schoenwiese (fair field in German), Silberfeld (silver field in German), Silver Plains, Sylvan (wooded), Wekusko (sweet grass in Cree), Zelena (green in Ukrainian), Zoria (star in Ukrainian, or rousing call at sunrise in Russian), Million (so called because of the optimistic spirit of the times), Happy Lake (named after two prospectors with Happy as their nicknames), Adelpha (brotherly/sisterly love in Greek),

Amaranth (unfading in Greek), Berry Patch, Bield (strong walk/shelter in Gaelic), Bloom, Blumengart (flower garden in German), Blumenort (flower nook in German), Cloverleaf Crocus, Fort Esperance (hope in French), Garden Island, Grande Point, Justice, Sweet Lake, and Zhoda (harmony/concord in Ukrainian), among others.

Perhaps less pleasant sounding place names should also be included here. Some of them are: Dismal Lake (north of Flin Flon), Drunken Lake (just west of Cross Lake), Bad Bache Rapids (today's Kilnabad Rapids on the Churchill River), the Lillesve community (Norwegian for small burnt place) is near Lundar, and Molson Lake was earlier called Little Winnipeg Lake (Winnipegosis Sakahigan means little nasty water lake in Algonquin).

B. SOURCES OF MANITOBA PLACE NAMES

CHURCHES AND MISSIONARIES

The following place names in Manitoba were named in honor of church leaders and/or missionaries: Arnaud, Beaudry, Budd, Camper, Camperville, Camp Morton, Carman, Charlebois, Dugas Point, Dufresne, Evans Point, Fairford, Flanders Lake, Fryer Point, Gallin Shoal, Giroux, Gonor, Lamb Lake, Lang, Langvale, McElheran, McGregor, Pomeroy, Ritchot, St. Vital, Spence, Wellwood, and Westbourne, among others.

Note: A number of place names honor Saints.

Note: At least 4252 families have been located and provided with Commemorative Name Certificates which state that members of Canada's World War II armed forces killed during that conflict have a Manitoba lake, river, or other location named in their honor.
See *UA Place of Honor*: "Manitoba's War Dead Commemorated in its Geography," 2nd Edition, edited by G.F. Holm and A.P. Buchner.

Explorers and Seamen

The following place names in Manitoba honor explorers and seamen: Anderson Point, Asham Point, Back Railway Point, Belcher, Bowsman, Button, Bylot, Cabot, Dufrost, Franklin, Gordon Point, Munk, Kelsey, Kellet, La Salle, Marquette, Medard Railway Point, Napper Lake, and Nelson Richard, among others.

Fur Trade

The following place names in Manitoba honor individuals attached to the fur trade: Aiken River, Alson Creek, Anderson Lake, Armit, Bayley Lake and Bay, Beale Creek, Beatty Creek, Berens River, Birds Hill, Bishop Lake, Bridges Railway Point, Chesnaye, Connolly Bay, Cook Lake, Cromarty, Demarch Lake, Douglas Lake, Fort Adhemar, Fort Ellice, Gillam, Girouard Lake, Hargrave Lake, Hayes River, Herman Lake, Lauder, Moar Lake, Monroe Point, McTavish, Médard, Niverville, Rockham Rock, Ross Iusland, Rossville, Simonhouse, and Warren Landing, among others.

Note: Nicholas Garry, Deputy Governor of the Hudson Bay Company (1822-35) "lent" his name to today's Fort Garry, part of Winnipeg, and to three earlier forts.

Royalty

The following place names in Manitoba honor royalty, vice-royalty, and aristocracy: Albert Beach, Baden, Bedford, Cauchon Lake, Cromer, Dauphin, Dynevor, Elgin, Fort Douglas, Fort Dufferin, Fort La Reine, Fort Maurepas, Fort Prince of Wales, Harmsworth, Harrowby, Jaroslaw, Lake Dauphin, Letellier, Lorne Lake, Louise Lake, Milner Ridge, Minto, Monominto, Morris, New Hirsch, Olha, Powell, Queen's Valley, Selkirk, Tolstoy, Victoria Beach, Waldersee, and York Factory, among others.

WOMEN

If women "hold up half the sky," why are there not more Manitoba place names honoring them? Here are some: Alfratta, Cantin Lake, Catherine (today's Letellier), Eleanor Lake, Elma, Ethelbert, Fannystelle, Findlay, Fort la Reine, Frances Lake, Frazerwood, Freedale, Garland, Glenella, Griswold, Hazel Railway Point, Ingelow, Isabella, Jenpeg, Kerfoot (today's Gregg), Ladywood, Lavinia, Louise Lake, Margaret, Melita, Mariapolis, Medord, Myra, Myrtle, Ninette, Ninga, Olha, Pruden, Queen's Valley, Reeder, Seven Sisters, Ste. Amélie, Ste. Anne, Ste. Elizabeth, Ste. Genevieve, Teulon, Vassar, Victoria Beach, and Willard, among others.

POLITICIANS

The following Manitoba places are named for politicians:

Agnew, Alexander, Amery, Argue, Banerman, Bedford, Benard, Beresford Lake, Bird, Bissette, Burnside, Carier, Carrick, Cartwright, Cromwell, Daly, Deacon, Dufrost, Drury Lake, Elphinstone, Fort Maruepas, Gervais Point, Gladstone, Goulet Lake, Greenway, Gunn Lake, Howden, Jacam, La Riviere, Laurier, Letellier, Lorne Lake, Lowe Farm, Lyddel, MacDonald, McCreary, McTavish, Melbourne, Milner Ridge, Morris, Nesbitt, Norris Lake, Rawebbe, Richer, Roblin Park, Roblin, Sanford, Scarth, Schaffner, Sewell, Sifton, Stitt, Ward, Waugh, and Winkler.

Note: Some names are placed in more than one category for obvious reasons.

SURVEYORS

The following Manitoba places are named for surveyors:
Abrey Lake, Allbright Lake, Alonsa, Amer Lake, Anderson Lake, Arden, Baldock Lake, Bayley Lake, Beatty Creek and Lake, Belcher, Bernie Lake, Bisgrove, Blank Lake, Bowden, Bowsman, Bridgar, Caddy Lake, Camp Whitney, Carbert Lake, Carroll Lake, Cartwright Lake, Cavanagh Lake, Christie Lake, Clarke Creek and Lake, Clausen Lake, Cotton Lake, Craven Lake, Currie Lake, Davidson Lake, Dawson Bay, Dennis Lake (see Dennis), Douglas Lake, Drybrough, Duval, Eaton Lake, Embury Lake, Evans Creek, Farwell Lake, Flett Lake, Ford Lake, Gammon River, Ganer Lake and River, Gilbert Lake, Gorainley Lake, Greenwood Lake, Harrison Creek, Harte Creek, Hayward Lake and Creek, Herman Lake, Herriott Island, Holcroft Lake, Holmes Lake, Howe Lake, Hughes Lake, Jetait Diustrict, Laronde Point, Last Lake, Lawledge, MacGillivray Lake, Molson Lake, Moore Lake, Morisette Lake and River, O'Hanly, Ogilvie (see Ogilvie), Ponton, Russell Lake, Settee Lake, Sharpe Lake, Strathclair, Thibaudeau, West Hawk Lake, Weston Pt., and Wrong, among others.

Note: Some of the rural post offices and railway points have long disappeared.

Aboriginal Names

Cree

Almasippi River, Anabusko River (Broad), Amista Asinee Island (Great Stone), Aniska Lake (Joining), Apeganau Lake (Big Bones), Apisko Lake (Elk), Apitsipi River (Fire Steel), Assaikwatami River (Flowing Backwads), Assapen Lake (Flying Squrrel), Asseen Lake and River (Stony), Aswapiswanon Lake (Watching for Swans), Athapap Beach (Rock on Both Sides), Atik Lake (Caribou), Atikamog Lake (Deer of the Lake), Atim (Dog), Aweme (I See You), Chacutinow Lake (Hill), Chemahawin Lake (Seine Net Fishing Clan), Cheman Lake (Canoe), Chitek Lake (Pelican), Chukitanaw (Hill), Echimanish River (Water Flowing Both Ways), Enatik Lake (White Spruce), Etomeni Falls (Water Flowing Both Ways), Fort Paskoyac (Weeded Narrows), Fort Pinacewaywinning (On the Way to the Ford on the Creek), Funisco Lake and River (Jackfish), Kanuchuam Rapids and River (Long Current), Kaskattema River (Unknown Translation), Kaupontekak Bay (Where the Spruce Meet), Kiskittogiso Lake (Cat), Kisseynew Lake (Old Man), Kississing Lake (Cold), Kwesitchewan Falls (Glittering Waters), Machichi River (Last), Manitou (Great Spirit), Maskawata (Oak Tree), Matago (Limestone), Mekiwin (Gift), Minago River (Spruce Tree), Minitonar (Hill Home of Little Gods), Miskow Lake (Red), Mispun (Snowing), Mistatim (Horse), Mistik Creek (Tree), Mistikokan River (Source Unknown), Mitas Point (Long Leggings), Moak Lake (Loon), Muhigan Lake (Wolf), Muskasew (Fox), Mukutawa River (Black), Namev Lake (Sturgeon), Nebogwenin Hill (Star Mound), Nueltin Lake (Windy), Oho River (Owl), Onatamini Brook (Berry Picking), Opachuanan Lake (Narrows), Opegama Lake (Pelvis Bones), Opiminegoka Lake (Narrow Spruce), Pakwa Lake (Chip), Paskquatchai River (Old Decayed Stump), Paungassi (Sandy Bar), Pawistik Rail Point (Waterfall), Pembina (Summerberry), Pennycutaway River

(Light the Fire), Peonan (Waiting Place), Pikwitone River (Broken Mouth), Pineimuta Lake (Partridge Crop), Pinesewachiwun River (It Flows Down), Pipun Rail Point (Winter), Sepastak (A Branch of a River), Shamattawa (Big Fork), Sepastik Creek (Channel River), Sipiwask (Lake of Many Channels), Sisib (Duck), Sispuk (Ducks), Sknowan (Turn Around), Tackinigue Falls (Split Rock Portage), Totogan (Low Swampy Land), Utik Lake (Deer), Wapisu Lake (Swan), Wapah (Strait), Washow Bay (Bay), Waskaiowake Lake (Turning Place), Wawanesa (Whipporwill?), Wekusko (Sweet Grass), Winnipegosis Lake (Little Lake of Dirty Water), Wuskwatin Lake (Beaver Dam).

Chippewa

Neepawa (Abundance), Ninga (Mother)

Ojibway

Animus (Dog)

Assinboine

Assinboine River (One Who Cooks Using Stones), Assinika Lake (Strong)

Sioux

Miniota (Water Plenty), Minnedosa (Flowing Water), Minnewasta Lake (Good Water), Napinka (Double).

C. Manitoba and Counting

If you ever wanted to count to fourteen in Cree, simply travel to Lake Payuk southeast of Flin Flon. There are fourteen lakes in a series. Here are their names and their "numbers":

1. Payuk, 2 Kanisota, 3 Nisto, 4 Nao, 5 Niyanum, 6 Nikotwasik, 7 Tapukok, 8 Uyenanao, 9 Kakat Mitatut, 10 Mitatut, 11 Paykosap, 12 Neosap, 13 Nistosap, 14 Naosap.

D. While You Are in Manitoba

You can find the three lakes called Ex, Wye, and Zed. Tired or celebrating surveyors used the alphabet to name those lakes east of Reindeer Lake.

You can swim in a lake called Ebb and Flow (Kakewekchewan in Cree means "where the current changes") situated southeast of Dauphin. The current comes from any change in the water level of Lake Manitoba. There are the Ebb and Flow Rapids on the Nelson River, as well. Turnagain Point is southeast of Reindeer Island.

You might rather choose the Pull and Be Damned Rapids on the Churchill River, where danger lurks because of the current.

Look for such place names as Knife Delta, Chisel Lake, Fork River, File Lake, Sickle Lake, Handle Lake, Kettle Rapids.

You can be well stung by wild bees while visiting the Kergwegan (means "town of bees" in Breton) district near McCreary. Manitoba can also boast of a Hornet Lake.

The Komarno Mosquito is actually a weather vane
Photo by Gerry Fox

Komarno, a village to the west and south of Gimli, has a "monument" constructed "to honor" the mosquitoes. Komar is Ukrainian for mosquito. (See photo, left). Keyes, a settlement east of Neepawa, was once known as Mosquito Lake. Morris River was earlier called Scratching Rover or Riviere aux Gratias. The small insect whose sharp sting leads to terrible itching is a "gratis." Near Newdale, there is a hill called Mosquito Mountain. Have you an itch to visit or revisit Manitoba?

Note that Mantricia on the Manitoba-Ontario border is a portmanteau word, combining Patricia (near Kenora) and Manitoba.

Also note that the Winnitoba rail point east of Whitemouth is a combination of Winnipeg and Manitoba.

Recognize that Mantario in the Whiteshell Provincial Park is a combination of Manitoba and Ontario.

Remember that Saskoba Lake is a combination of Saskatchewan and Manitoba. So is Saskman, a lake near Sherridon.

Observe that many people claim that Marquette, near Portage la Prairie, is halfway (midpoint) across Canada east-to-west. The famed explorer, navigator and map-maker Jacques Marquette (1637-75) is honored by the village's name.

Will you listen to the clergy who might tell you that the church service you attended was based on the Book of Acts 28:1, which tells of St. Paul's ship being wrecked on the island called Melita, today's Malta? That account is the source of the settlement's name – near Deloraine – according to some sources.

Hunt for Moose Head Mountain, Moose Island, Moose Nose Lake, Moose Nose Rail Point, Moosehorn, North Moose Lake, Moosehorn Bay (today's Silver Bay near Fairford).

You might be told that a coin toss determined that the village near Killarney was called Cartwright in honor of Sir Richard Cartwright, an early Dominion minister of finance. Had the coin "come up tails," the village would have been called Caledon. Earlier, the settlement was called Badger Creek. Take your choice.

Note that Cram Creek flows into Lake Manitoba from the south. If you are subject to cramps, perhaps you should stay away. Cramps, so named after an individual with that name, was later misspelled, i.e., "Cram."

Remember that the Russo-Japanese War (1904-05) lent names to Manitoba. Dalny, near Deloraine, was named after the Chinese port of Dalny, a place prominent in that war, which eventually ended with the Treaty of Portsmouth.

Makaroff, northeast of Dauphin, was named in honor of the Russian Vice-Admiral Makaroff, who went down with his ship, which was accidentally torpedoed by his countrymen. Incidentally, Togo, a neighboring village just inside the Saskatchewan border, was named after the Japanese hero, Admiral Togo.

Remember that Dot, near Whitemouth, was a dot on the map, so to add a little class, the community on the CPR line changed its name to Decimal.

Ask if a Greek scholar named Alpha, Beta, and Gamma.

"Will you have a drop more [of whiskey]?" an early farmer supposedly asked an important visitor, who then declared: "We will call this place Dropmore." It is near Grandin.

You might make a very slow trip to Starbuck, a bit west of Winnipeg. It seems that the settlement was named after two oxen, Star and Buck.

Dance at Pruden Bay, north of Winnipeg, where according to legend the most beautiful girl of the old Red River district was yanked home by her father because she had danced "a wicked polka."

Visit Devil Island, at the mouth of the Winnipeg River. Earlier natives believed that "if you point at Devil Island, you won't get home tonight."

Leave northward from Amery near Gillam, and you'll be entering the Land of Big Sticks.

Holiday in Arizona, a district east of Brandon.

Be advised: Artery Lake drains into the Bloodvein River.

Bring your culinary skills to the shore of the Assiniboine River. In Cree, Assini means "stone," and boine means "one who cooks."

Picnic on old Baldy Mountain in Duck Mountain Provincial Park. Oxygen tanks are not required on the 2 727-kilometer mountain.

Start at Arona railway point west of Portage la Prairie. Then "follow the alphabet," i.e., Bloom, Caye, Deer, Exira, Firdale, and more, until you reach Yorko and Zenata in Saskatchewan.

Check out the names of ships and seamen carved on rocks in Sloop Cove on Churchill River. It is claimed that one etching is of a man hanged for stealing a goose.

Reread the legend involving the bittersweet romance and loss as described by the famous Indian poetess, Pauline Johnson. A young voyageur traveling on a river kept hearing his name being called by a lovely female voice. The young man repeatedly answered, "Who calls?" or "Qu'Appelle": the name now for the Qu'Appelle River, a tributary of the Assiniboine River.

Note that the name Winnipeg first appeared on page one of the "Nor'Wester," February 24, 1886. In Cree, winnepeg is win-nipiy, meaning murky water.

E. There's More in Manitoba

Sobe Creek flows from the west into Grass River. Sobe is short for "son of a bitch," a term given by the some miners who lost some equipment in the creek.

In Manitoba, you can find Turtle Mountain. Nearby Boissevain has featured the famous turtle derby.

Waskada, near Deloraine, comes from the native Wa-sta-daow, which means "better further on," an expression used by Indians to entice white settlers to move from the area.

The Boer War (1899-1902) produced place names for Manitoba. Powell, named for the defender of Mafeking and the founder of the Boy Scout Movement, Lord Baden-Powell, is a railway point north and a bit east of Swan River. Nearby is another railway point, Baden. The settlement called Mafeking is further south. The Boer War battle at Ladysmith is remembered by the railway point so named near Portage la Prairie (see Lord Baden-Powell).

South Africa is further remembered by Milner Ridge near Selkirk. Milner was High Commissioner for South Africa before, during, and after the Boer War. A bit south of Swan River is Durban, named after the South African city of that name.

Libreville, an early Manitoba post office, took its name from the Congo district of Africa.

Firdale, west of Portage la Prairie, was once called China.

Manitoba's sea port, Churchill, was known as Munk's Harbor in honor of the ill-fated Danish explorer who visited the site in 1619. Scurvy killed sixty-one of Munk's crew.

Because surveyors did their work there on election day, they called it Election Lake, near Flin Flon.

The Findlay district near Virden lost the entire Leitch family at the terrible Frank Slide disaster in southwest Alberta, April 29, 1903. The visiting family were buried under countless large boulders. Findlay was Mrs. Alex Leitch's maiden name. The area was named in honor of those victims.

High Bluff, just east of Portage la Prairie, where the unrecognized Republic of Caledonia was created by its president, Thomas Spence in 1867. Spence wrote to Queen Victoria, who was asked to recognize the "republic." No response. So Spence changed the name to the Republic of Manitoba with High Bluff as its capital. The president and his cronies collected tariffs and allegedly spent the money on liquid sunshine. A shoemaker named MacPherson challenged the often-drunk Spence. A trial emerged, and a first-rate fist fight took place there and then. MacPherson was found guilty of "treason to the laws of the republic." By summer of 1868, London officials informed the republic that it had no power or legal existence. The republic disappeared. Later, Spence served in Louis Riel's provisional government.

Buchan, Osborne, Russell, Muckle Creek, Powell, Baden, Waldersee, Peterson district, among others, are named for military men. Katrime, near Neepawa, was earlier called Wellington Plains, after the British general who defeated Napoleon.

Winnipeg means murky water because, as the legend reports, Lake Winnipeg and Lake Winnipegosis have demons living in their depths. Those demons stir up the water, making it muddy.

Near Churchill is Never Fails Island, so named by hungry HBC workers hunting for ptarmigan which were then in abundance there.

The oak has been popular in Manitoba. Consider these place names: Oak Bluff, Oak Hammock, Oak Island, Oak Lake, Oak Point, Oak River, Oakland, Oakley, Oakner, Oaknook, Oakview, Oakville. Another settlement near Winnipeg, Prairie Grove, was earlier known as Coteau des Chênes or Oak Knoll. The Des Chenes (south of Winnipeg) translates to Oak Island.

At the entrance to Riding Mountain National Park was a post office built on a knoll. The office's name: Onanole.

Artifacts and trade items from Mexico were found in a mound, mepawaquemoshen (meaning little dance hill, after the ceremonial dances), near today's Pilot Mound.

Because Saskatchewan means rapid river, the settlement north of Brandon was nearly called Saskatchewan City instead of today's Rapid City.

Many experts claim that Roland, south and west of Winnipeg, is where Canada's 4-H movement was born.

The names of four mining officials joined to make the railway point Roblaytin: Roche (Ro), Blake (B), Ayre (Ay), and Austin (Tin).

There are approximately three dozen Manitoba place names beginning with St. or Ste. Examples: St. Vital and Ste. Anne. Over twenty place names start with Fort. Examples: Fort Garry and Fort Assiniboine.

Thompson, named after John F. Thompson, President of the International Nickel Company, has often been called "Manitoba's Instant City."

Wawanesa was once called Sipweski: pronounced "sip of whiskey."

Calico Island was named after a river steamer which was destroyed in 1892 on the Saskatchewan River rapids. A large shipment of calico was rescued and set out to dry on the island.

Airplanes and their pilots have made history in Manitoba. In 1923, Flying Officer Clayton of the RCAF landed on this lake and named it after himself. Aeronica Lake in the Duck Mountain Provincial Park is named after an Aeronica airplane that crashed nearby. Costes Lake takes its name from a French pilot. Costello Lake was named after another pilot. The Guynemer District northeast of Dauphin honors another French pilot. Amphibian Lake took its name from a type of aircraft used in photographing northern Manitoba. Bennett, west of Selkirk, was named after airman Floyd Bennett. Edmund Lake is named for Edmund Norris, a pilot killed while flying a group of people to God's Lake. The railway point called Stall Lake honors a bush pilot named Stall. Stevenson Island was named after a pilot was killed in 1928 while flying near The Pas. Small Lake is named for a member of the Manitoba Government Air Service. Another pilot is remembered by the naming of the Hone district. Hobbs Lake, near the Ontario border, was named after a RCAF pilot. A pilot named Guthrie, a man who photographed the area, had Guthrie Lake named after him. Cobham River is named after Sir Allan Cobham, a British airman (1929).

While in Manitoba, think roses, and consider some of the province's place names: Rosebank (near Morden), Roseland (near Brandon), Rosenort (southwest of Winnipeg), Rosenhoff (south of Winnipeg), Rosenfeld (near Emerson), Rosengart (near Morden), and Rosenburg (near Hodgson), among others.

East of Brandon lies the village of Sidney, which once experienced a buffalo stampede down its main street.

Swan River was once the legislative headquarters of the North West Territories.

Oxford Lake, west of God's Lake, used to be called Holy Lake, a translation of the native Petepaw Nippi. That name means "lake with a hole in the bottom." Natives believed that it was a route to another world.

St. Andrews Lake was named for the patron saint of Scotland. St. Patrick Lake, for the patron saint of Ireland.

St. David Lake was named for the patron saint of Wales. (All three are located a bit north of the Fisher River Indian Reserve, near the west coast of Lake Winnipeg.) St. George, a lake and a village near Pine Falls, was named for the patron saint of England. St. Joseph, northwest of Emerson, named in honor of the patron saint of Canada. Ste. Anne, southeast of Winnipeg, honored the patron saint of Brittany, France. Perhaps St. Genevieve, an earlier post office southeast of Winnipeg, was named to honor the patron saint of Paris. St. Jean Baptiste, northwest of Emerson, was named to honor the patron saint of French Canadians.

An earlier name for the Churchill River was River-of-Strangers, so named by Indians who found the bodies of the Danish crew led by explorer Munk. The natives also found supplies on board, such as tools, medicines, gunpowder, and mirrors. They attempted to "dry out" the gunpowder over a fire (they didn't know about the danger). The explosion killed many of the Indians. Some experts call the event a legend.

Visit Fort Dufferin (Emerson) where the remarkable and famous march west of the North West Mounted Police began. It was an impressive sight when the NWMP departed Fort Dufferin around 5 p.m. on July 9. The tight column stretched back more than four kilometers and consisted of 274 Mounties (including one surgeon and eleven veterinary surgeons), twenty Métis guides, and 310 horses, followed by a collection of other animals and equipment that included two mortars, two one-ton cannons, 114 oxcarts, seventy-three wagons, thirty-three head of beef cattle, 142 work oxen, forges, mowing machines, farming equipment, ploughs, and more.[1]

---

1 Elle Andra-Warner. *The Mounties*. Canmore: Altitude. 2004, p. 46. The numbers and items noted above have not always found agreement among writers and historians. For example, see Colin A. Thomson. *Swift Runner*. Calgary: Detselig. 1983, p. 34.

F. After the Violence . . .

Bull Island near Norway House was so named because an angry bull gored and stomped postmaster Thomas Isbister to death at the Nelson River post. The chief factor at Norway House had the bull shot and carried to the island, where the carcass was burned. The fire got out of control, and it burned most of the island's vegetation.

Cromarty, a railway point south of Churchill, honors an HBC factor who was killed by Indians at Fort Severn.

Hudson Bay, so much a part of Manitoba's history, was named after Henry Hudson (c. 1550-1611), explorer and navigator who sought the northwest passage to China and the Far East. Hudson, his twelve-year old son, and seven other souls were set in an open boat by mutineers. The cold waters of Hudson Bay likely claimed them, because they were never seen again. Historians have been slow to call the mutiny murder. (See Hudson.)

La Salle, a cannon shot southwest of Winnipeg, is another Manitoba settlement named in honor of a murdered man. René Robert Cavalier Sieur de La Salle (1643-87), was born in Rouen, France. As a young man, he settled near Montreal as a trader. As an explorer, he descended the Ohio and Mississippi Rivers to the sea (Gulf of Mexico) in 1682. He claimed lands for France and named the area Louisiana, then a huge area extending to the border of Canada. He explored parts of Louisiana (named in honor of King Louis XIV), and spent two years of fruitless search for the Mississippi Delta. His men mutinied and La Salle was slaughtered.

Massacre Island, in the Lake of the Woods, is well named. On June 8, 1736, Sioux Indians killed twenty-one people there, including the missionary Father Aulneau. Some torture was involved. Named in the priest's honor, Arnaud (misspelled for Aulneau) is a settlement east and north of Emerson.

Semple is the name of a river, a lake, and a community named in honor of the governor of the HBC, who, with twenty colonists, was slain at the famous Massacre of Seven Oaks, in June of 1816. The British officer and the others were killed in battle with Cuthbert Grant's group of Nor'Westers.

Warren Landing, near Norway House, is named after one John Warren of the HBC. He was shot by some Nor'Westers a few years before the 1821 amalgamation of the North West Company and the HBC.

Some experts claim that Slave Falls, north and east of Winnipeg, is named to honor a Sioux maiden who was captured by the Salteaux. She escaped, only to drown herself there.

It took the jury eight minutes to render a verdict of guilty: Charcoal, murderer of NWMP Sgt. William Wilde and a Blood Indian, Medicine Pipe Stem, was hanged at Fort Macleod on February 10, 1897. Still weak from his attempted suicide – by slashing his wrists – he could not stand, so was hanged sitting on a chair. He sang his death song all the way to the scaffold. It had taken 100 police and six dozen aboriginals to catch him. The Wilde railway point, named in honor of Sgt. Wilde, was on the CNR line and due east of Thompson.

While window shopping in Paris on May 25, 1926, Symon Petlura was assassinated by a Jewish anarchist named Sholom Schwartzbard, who, after firing the three shots, calmly handed his gun to the police while saying: "You can arrest me, I've killed a murderer." Petlura (or Petliura 1879-1926) was a leader of Ukraine's unsuccessful fight for independence following the 1917 Russian Revolution. The controversial statesman, socialist politician, army veteran, editor, writer, and founder of the Ukrainian Labor Party was briefly the President of Ukraine during the Russian Civil War. Petlura was accused by many people, including his assassin, of participating in the pogroms which murdered tens of thousands of Jews in eastern Europe. Schwartzbard told the court that fifteen family members had been killed during the pogroms, and that he was simply avenging those victims. The French jury acquitted him. Petlura, a community near Grandview, was named in honor of the Ukrainian nationalist.

One of the most distinctive historical site markers in Manitoba is located at the junctions of Highways No. 1 and 26. The striking white horse catches your attention, and the plaque gives you the legend of Indian warfare, tragic love, and a ghostly white horse roaming the plain. After an angry, jealous suitor killed "his" fleeing sweetheart and her new husband, the woman's white horse continued to roam the area, free and untamed. That Indian legend led to the naming of White Horse Plains, today's St. François Xavier, west of Winnipeg. A statue of a white horse greets visitors to the community (see photo below).

Source: Manitoba Historical Society, Historical Tour: Highway 26, by Rosemary Malaher.

The old man was attacked with swords and spears. He experienced a horrible death. The martyr had his name honored as a Manitoba place name, St. Boniface (see St. Boniface).

J.E. Tail died from his wound late in World War I. He was awarded the Victoria Cross and Military Medal for Bravery. The Jetait district, south of Lynn Lake, is named in his honor. Cracknell, north of Russell, was named in honor of Edward Cracknell, who was awarded the Military Medal during World War I.

Some writers insist that on Sunday, May 30, 1897, the last Indian vs White battle took place, not far from where Louis Riel, Gabriel Dumont, and followers lost the famous Battle of Batoche to the forces of General Frederick Dobson Middleton twelve years earlier.

The 1897 battle featured a twenty-one-year old Cree named Almighty Voice, his nineteen-year old cousin named Tupean, and the thirteen-year old Salteaux named Standing-in-the-Sky, pitted against over 100 police officers and volunteers.

The literary icon Pierre Berton offered this summary:

> Almighty Voice murdered three Mounted Police men in the performance of their duty, murdered a white civilian and maimed three others. He lured two teenagers to their deaths – one a child of thirteen – and was the cause of a furious gun battle. If he had been a white kid from the city slums, he would have gone down in history as a mad-dog killer . . .[1]

In 1895, Almighty Voice – or Koh-kee-say-man-e-too-wayo – was arrested for stealing and killing a steer. The young man escaped custody, only to "touch off the tragedy and led, obliquely, to ten deaths . . ."[2] He was "tribal married" at age sixteen to a thirteen-year old neighbor girl. By the time of his final days, he was "still working on wife number four."

In October, 1895, NWMP Sergeant Colin Campbell Colebrook, a thrity-three-year-old Englishman, was ordered to recapture Almighty Voice. The native shot Colebrook in the neck. He fell dead from his horse. Small Face, the native girl bride, witnessed the shooting.

For nineteen months Almighty Voice could not be found.

A reward was offered for his capture. The murderer and his two young companions were spotted in a small poplar bluff in the Minichinas Hills, close to Saskatchewan's One Arrow Reserve.

Police Inspector John B. Allan, who preferred to be called Bronco Jack, was shot in the arm by Almighty Voice. Before receiving treatment, Allan placed Corporal C.H.S. Hockin in charge. (Allan's one-hour operation produced a saucerful of bone splinters; no anaesthetic was available.)

The thirty-seven-year-old Hockin, an ex-British Army officer and son of an Admiral, should have known better.

Almighty Voice, Cree leader, in the Duck Lake area, Saskatchewan, around 1892-94
Courtesy Glenbow Archives
NA-2301-1.

About 6:30 p.m., at intervals of eight yards, nine men led by Hockin "combed" the bluff. A shot rang out. Postmaster Grundy, a volunteer, was shot in the abdomen. He died immediately. Another rifle shot caught Hockin in the chest, and he fell to the ground. "Oh, God, I'm shot." He uttered. His men dragged him from the bush. The officer died the next morning.

Reinforcements and heavy guns came by train to the site from Regina (see Herchmer). Other help arrived from Prince Albert. Round after round of rifle fire were sent through the bluff of trees. Heavy guns added to the situation.

The three young natives were found dead. The bombardment had been successful. Later, the bluff of trees was cut down, and the earth was ploughed into farmland.

Legends were born from Almighty Voice's life and death. Some writers romanticized the man and the battle. Berton responded: "For surely it is a libel on any race to suggest that a twenty-one-year-old punk is the best it can produce."[3]

Earlier, the *Toronto Globe* offered this assessment: "Almighty Voice was a bad Indian, but he had the stuff in him of which heroes are made."

Meanwhile, men like Hockin, Colebrook, and others are largely forgotten. A sad commentary, indeed. A railway point south of Thompson was named in his honor.

---

1 Pierre Berton. *The Legend of Almighty Voice: The Wild Frontier.* Toronto: Bantam Books, 1980. p. 218.
2 Ibid.
3 Ibid.

Selected Bibliography

Aiken, Don. *It Happened In Manitoba*. Calgary: Fifth House, 2004.

Andra-Warner, Elle. *The Mounties*. Canmore: Altitude , 2004

Baker, Jean H. *Sisters: The Lives of American's Suffragists*. New York: Hill and Wang, 2005.

Berton, Pierre. *Klondike: The Last Great Gold Rush 1896-1899*. Toronto: McClelland & Stewart Inc., 1972.

Berton, Pierre. *The Wild Frontier*. Toronto: McClelland and Stewart, 1980.

Bordin, Ruth. *Frances Willard: A Biography*. Chapel Hill, UNC Press, 1986.

Bowsfield, Hartwell. *Louis Riel: The Rebel and The Hero*. Toronto: Oxford University Press, 1971.

Brown, George W. et al (Eds). *Dictionary of Canadian Biography*. Toronto: University of Toronto Press, various dates.

Colombo, John Robert. *Colombo's New Canadian Quotations*. Edmonton: Hurtig Publishers, 1987.

Commire, Anne (Ed). *Women In World History: A Biographical Encyclopedia*. New York: Yorkin Publications, 2000.

Douglas, Robert. *Place Names of Manitoba*. Ottawa: Kings Printer, N.D.

Drabble, Margaret (Ed). *The Oxford Companion to English Literature*. Oxford: Oxford University Press, 2000.

Dugas, Georges. *The Canadian West*. (English translation of 1905). Montreal: Librairie Beauchemin, 1905.

Francis, R. Douglas and Palmer, Howard (Eds). *The Prairie West: Historical Readings*. Edmonton: Pica Pica Press, 1985.

Green, Jonathon. *Cassell Dictionary of Cynical Quotations*. London: Cassell Co., 1999.

Ham, Penny. *Place Names of Manitoba*. Saskatoon: Western Producer Prairie Books, 1980.

Hamilton, William B. *The Macmillan Book of Canadian Place Names*. Toronto: Macmillan of Canada, 1978.

Hargrave, Joseph James. *Red River*. Montreal: John Lovell, 1871.

Howard, Joseph Kinsey. *Strange Empire: The Story of Louis Riel*. Toronto: Swan Publishing, 1952.

Knowles, Elizabeth (ed). *The Oxford Dictionary of Quotations (6 Ed)*. New York: Oxford University Press, 2004.

Macleod M.A. and Morton, W.L. *Cuthbert Grant of Grantown.* Toronto: McClelland & Stewart, 1963.

McGovern, Una. *Chambers Biographical Dictionary.* Edinburgh: Chambers Harrap, 2002.

Metcalf, Fred (Ed). *The Penguin Dictionary of Modern Humorous Quotations.* London: Penguin Books, 2001.

Morton, W.L. *Manitoba: A History.* Toronto: University of Toronto Press, 1957.

Ratcliffe, Susan (Ed). *The Oxford Dictionary of Thematic Quotations.* Oxford: Oxford University Press, 2000.

Rees, Nigel (Ed). *Cassell Companion To Quotations.* London: Cassell Publishers, 1997.

Ross, Alexander. *The Red River Settlement.* Edmonton: Hurtig Publishers, 1972.

Rudnycky, J.B. *Manitoba Mosaic of Place Names.* (Photocopy, N.D.)

The Dictionary of Canadian Biography. Toronto: University of Toronto Press, various dates.

The Canadian Encyclopedia, Vol. I, II, III, IV. Edmonton: Hurtig Publishers, 1988.

Thomson, Colin. *The Romance of Alberta Settlements.* Calgary: Detselig Enterprises, 2004.

Thomson, Colin A. *Swift Runner.* Calgary: Detselig Enterprises, 1984.

Thomson, Colin and Prindle, F. Lee. *Sounds Like Albrerta.* Calgary: Detselig Enterprises Ltd., 2006.

Thomson, Colin and Rodney. *The Romance of Saskatchewan Settlements.* Prince Albert: Thoro, 2005.

Thomson, George Malcolm. *The North-West Passage.* London, Futura Publications, 1975.

Trémandan, A.H. *Hold High Your Heads.* Elizabeth D. Magvet, trans. Winnipeg, Pemmican Publishers, 1982.

Ward, Laura. *Famous Last Words.* London: PRC Publishing, 2004

Williams, D.C. and Richmond, S. *Canada: Colony to Centennial.* Toronto: McGraw-Hill Co. of Canada Ltd., 1970.

Map 1 of Manitoba

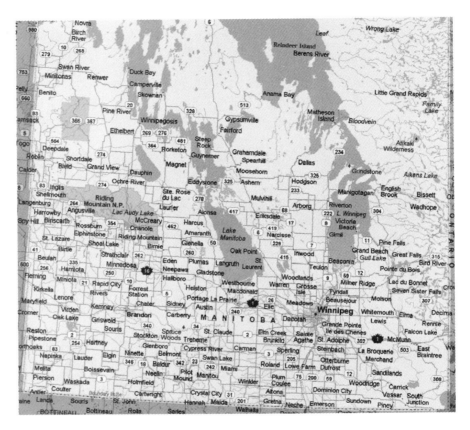

Manitoba Road Map (South)
Source: Electronic. http://mapz411.ca/maps/mb_south.asp

Map 2 of Manitoba

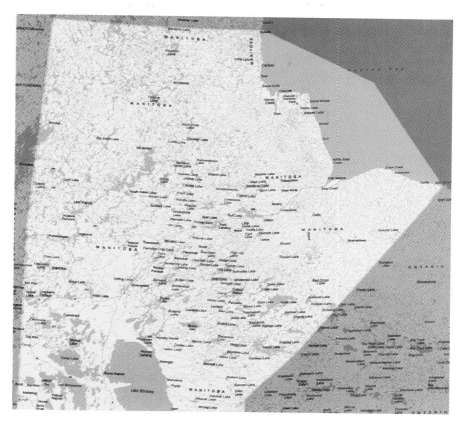

Manitoba Road Map (North)
Source: Electronic. http://mapz411.ca/maps/mb_north.asp
s.